STALKED

STALKED

A TRUE STORY

I Was Stalked and Raped by the Same Man Twice…and the System Didn't Protect Me

by
LA VONNE SKALIAS
with
BARBARA DAVIS

THE SUMMIT GROUP • FORT WORTH, TEXAS

THE SUMMIT GROUP
1227 West Magnolia, Suite 500, Fort Worth, Texas 76104

Printed in the United States of America.

10   9   8   7   6   5   4   3   2   1

Library of Congress Cataloging-in-Publication Data

Skalias, La Vonne, 1946–

    Stalked: a true story / by La Vonne Skalias with Barbara Davis.

    p. cm.

    ISBN 1-56530-146-3: $19.95

    1. Skalias, Lavonne, 1946– . 2. Rape victims—Texas—Case studies. 3.

Stalking—Texas—Case studies. I. Davis, Barbara, 1951- . II. Title.

HV6565.T4S57 1994

364.1'532'092—dc20

[B}   94-26270

                                                           CIP

To the most high God, my keeper of the flame; and to my
beloved cousin Linda, for all of her fervent prayers.
-La Vonne Skalias

To the memory of my beloved sister, Linda McNabb Bush.
-Barbara Davis

Table of Contents

PART III TAKING CONTROL

Acknowledgments

LA VONNE SKALIAS

I thank my family, and the many friends, coworkers, volunteers, and professionals who have offered me their support, information, and help through this ordeal, including: Raven Kazen, State Director for Victims Services at the Texas Department of Criminal Justice and a volunteer with the Austin Chapter of People Against Violent Crimes, founded by Nell Myers; Rona Stratton Smith, advocate for the Families of Murdered Victims; JoAnn Shaffer, program director and advocate of National Victim Center; Deborah Caddy, Director of Rape Crisis of Tarrant County; Dr. Jerry Harris, founder of Families of Murdered Victims; Texas Council on Family Violence; Rex Henderson, Fort Worth Crime Commissioner; and victims' advocates Ray Stewart, Linda Braswell Sullivan, David Sullivan, Linda Barker-Lowrance, Kay Day, Al and Jerry Foster, members of Victims of Violence; and Sherry Shanafeldt and the support staff of Victims Assistance of Tarrant County.

I also thank the late Christy Bennett, who worked tirelessly to help victims and their families, and her husband David, who was our anchor; Bonnie, my first Rape Crisis volunteer, who, throughout my pain, was a ray of sunshine; Janet Halbert, my little angel of mercy, and Jane Bingham, a minister, advocate, and powerhouse for victims' rights, both of Rape Crisis; District Attorney Tim Curry, for his attention, support, and tenacious efforts to bring about justice; Alan Levy, my special high priest; David Montague and Mike Parrish, for not giving up on Michelle and me; Karen Kalergis, director of the Governor's Office Texas Crime Victims Clearinghouse; the wonderful advocates of We the People in Harlingen, Texas; to Ronnie and Pam, a special thank-you; Jeffrey, my "special agent"; Sharon, Carolyn, and Ruth, for giving me sanctuary; Fern Gant, for her wisdom and strength; the Recent Victims Support Group, for their love and teaching victims how to "open up"; those who were so thoughtful to remember me with the lovely Sunshine Basket; the medical staff at John Peter Smith Hospital; and Barbara Davis, the little lady who saved my life.

I thank Rosalind Wright and Sherry Selvage, two writers supportive of my story.

I thank the many groups who offered their prayers, including: the Bible study group at work for their prayers, love, and support; Tom, Helene, Michael, Velma, Kay, Gloria, Judy, Sandy, Robbie, and Clara; Cookie, who knows how to make me laugh; my bosses and coworkers, who have been patient on the bad days and supportive on the good days; Margaret and Chuck, who helped me walk out of the past into the present; Bill, Marlene, Anita, Pastor Doug, Lary, and Bible study members for their positive, encouraging words; David, who wrote a song, "The Hiding Place," for us; Betty and Tommy for their special prayers; Ruth, a courageous lady and good Samaritan; the pastors and members of Haltom Road Baptist Church, Bethesda Community Church, Restoration Church, and The Church on the Rock in Palestine, Texas.

I thank Governor Ann Richards for signing the Anti-Stalking Bill for past and present victims, such as myself.

Thank you to State Representative Brian McCall and State Senator Mike Moncrief, for their tireless efforts in persuading enough representatives and senators to vote for the Anti-Stalking Bill to pass the House and Senate and find its way to the Governor's desk.

And last, but dearest to my heart, I thank my family: Mom and Dad for their undying love, support, and prayers; my Aunt Ann and Uncle Tony for their love and support; and my daughter, Michelle, who travelled this road with me—you will always be my baby.

BARBARA DAVIS

I thank the following people for their help and support:

Dr. R. L. (Leon) Rhodes for guiding me through the path of La Vonne's medical history, and for his patience and guidance in reading my work while managing to stay my best friend.

My family, beginning with my husband, Jim, whose infinite patience, belief in me, and acceptance of many TV dinners helped me make my deadline; my daughter Lisa and my son Troy, for letting their mom take time from them to finish this book; my parents, Bill and Thelma McNabb, for giving up my company on many occasions so I could finish this project, and for understanding what it meant to me.

My two close friends, Ken Dies and Lawrence Smith, for being gentle but truthful while nursing me along, telling me to hang in there, and encouraging me to believe in what I was doing.

My dear friend, Lawton Williams, who always had faith in me and taught me I could do anything I put my mind to.

DFW Writer's Association for the wisdom and knowledge they passed my way and their honesty in helping me tell a story that needed to be told.

Finally, above all, I'd like to thank and acknowledge La Vonne Skalias and her daughter, Michelle, for allowing me into their lives and opening up to me the depths of their souls, to show the world what it really feels like to be victimized, and how one can triumph and overcome the adversities in his or her life.

Introduction

In 1977, La Vonne Skalias's primary concern is making ends meet and being a good parent to her five-year-old daughter, Michelle. La Vonne has no idea that she is about to embark upon an odyssey that will span a decade, and fill her with a terror few ever know.

La Vonne's existence takes an irreversible course when eighteen-year-old Lanny Bevers enters her life in early September 1974. At the time, she is married to Michelle's father, George, who hires some neighborhood boys to work on a landscaping project in the Skaliases' backyard. Lanny's brother, Mike, is one of these young men.

In contrast to La Vonne's introverted nature, George is an extrovert and can be seen regularly in the front yard chatting with neighbors and working on the lawn. Lanny and Mike stop by occasionally and say a few friendly words to George. Sometimes, Lanny is by himself when he stops to talk to George.

Shortly after the landscaping project is finished, the Skaliases begin receiving anonymous telephone calls. In the beginning, only country and western music plays in the background. The calls soon evolve into obscene messages. The messages are sporadic for the first few months, then start coming closer together.

On December 18, 1974, agitated, George requests Southwestern Bell to place a tap on the phone to locate the origin of the calls. It remains for the two-week period the phone company allows, without any results. Over the next few years, the calls come intermittently. The Skaliases consider it a mere annoyance.

By 1977, La Vonne is divorced, a single parent, and employed by a local school district as the receptionist and secretary to the assistant superintendent.

Thursday, June 23, 1977, is a typical, hot Texas summer day. Nothing in the air hints of the emotional upheaval ahead. A reign of terror is about to descend on La Vonne that does not cease until the fall of 1988, and which will place her in the national spotlight.

La Vonne Skalias is not an extraordinary human being, by her definition. Those who know her, and those of us who have come to know her, will argue differently.

Note from the Publisher

Portions of this book are very graphic. Excerpts from the trials and tapes used in this book are reproduced verbatim from the court records. Addresses have been changed, and, where noted, names have been changed to protect those involved.

Prologue

Gasping desperately to breathe, La Vonne is certain she is suffocating. A man's hand is tightly clamped over La Vonne's mouth and nose, choking off her passage of air. She frantically pries the hand away, eagerly gulping for air. Her head, aching from the temporary loss of oxygen, turns toward the intruder. His features are grossly distorted, like a monster in a freak show. A stocking tightly bound around his head is knotted at the side of the neck. Uncertain of what the intruder wants, La Vonne is filled with terror.

His hot breath on her neck sends shivers down her spine as he whispers in her ear, "It's payback time, bitch!" The words—"payback time"—resonate through her mind. With the realization this is Lanny Bevers, nausea wells in the pit of her stomach, threatening to spew forth its contents.

Her mind races wildly; thoughts of daughter Michelle's safety intrude, as she strives for a measure of control. The contemplation that he has harmed her child strikes a cord of terror deep within her. Her thoughts are interrupted as she is turned on her back, her chest straddled, her arms secured against the bed. Horror envelops her as the glistening blade of a butcher knife is lifted high into the air. A blood-curdling scream erupts from the depths of her soul, shattering the still of the night.

Whimpering like a child pleading not to be punished, she begs, "Don't...don't do this...please, don't do this..." Her plea is ignored, as the blade plunges into the center of her chest. Blood gushes from the wound, while she struggles violently to survive. Her body lurches forward as the weapon, wielded in a frenzy, cuts into her repeatedly. The intruder's laughter satiates the room, as La Vonne's life slowly drains from her body.

Panic intermingles with excruciating pain as thoughts of her child permeate her mind. "Michelle," she murmurs, "Michelle." Her voice softly trails off, silenced by the intrusion of the knife thrust one last time into her.

Fading into the obscurity that awaits, her candle flickers out, as her final thoughts rest with her child...her beautiful child.

La Vonne Skalias jolts upright in bed as her sweat-soaked body continues to tremble. Disorientated and frightened, she feels her heart pound like a drum. Slowly, her senses are aroused as she tries to separate fact from fantasy.

Under her breath, she curses the nightmare that continues to haunt her. Shivering, she wraps her arms around her legs and pulls her knees to her chest. In an effort to regain her composure, she rocks herself back and forth. Searching the room for any remnant of her dream, she finds none. Bevers is not here.

Reality returns to mollify her tormented soul. Remembering her nemesis is securely incarcerated in the Coffield Unit of the Texas Department of Corrections, La Vonne relaxes, settling back against the softness of her pillow. Scooting down in the bed, she pulls the covers tightly up around her neck and lets out a deep sigh of relief.

Everything is all right. He's not here…not tonight, anyway. Attempting to fall back to sleep, she is distressed by the knowledge that the dream will return.

She is as certain of this as she is that Lanny Bevers will return, to fulfill his promise to finish the job he'd started almost sixteen years earlier.

Part I

The Beginning

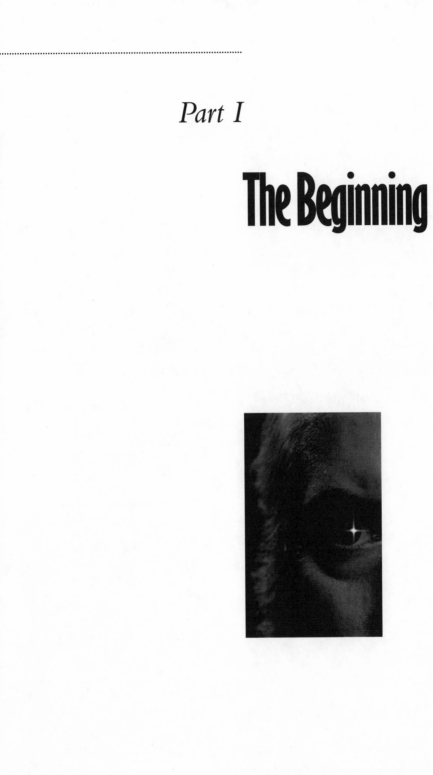

Chapter 1

Night of Terror

Thursday is a tough day at work. Tired from the long day, I leave the office and pick up Michelle at the day-care center. Once home, Michelle and I play for a while, then I give her a coloring book to occupy her as I prepare dinner. After dinner, I wash the dishes and await the arrival of my boyfriend, Brad Stephens.

Brad and I have been dating for the last year-and-a-half. He is a teacher at the local junior college. His routine is to come by on Tuesdays, Thursdays, and Fridays to visit. Around 8:00 P.M., Brad calls and says he will not be able to make it tonight. I am disappointed.

I put Michelle to bed around 9:00 P.M. and decide to retire early myself. Living alone with a small child, I have become extremely cautious about locking the house. As usual, I make my nightly rounds of double-checking all the doors to make sure they are locked.

As I lock the kitchen door that adjoins the garage, I briefly reflect that once again the garage doors will be closed but not locked. The automatic garage door opener had broken several months earlier. Unable to motivate any of the men in my life (boyfriend, father, or uncle) to repair it, I was making do with a broomstick to secure the doors. But the broom, too, had broken. Weariness overtakes me. I sigh out loud and think, I can't worry about everything.

As I walk back to the bedroom, I pause to check on Michelle. Her room is just off the hall, close to mine. I quietly open her bedroom door so I will be able to hear her during the night. I peek in. She is sound asleep.

I climb into bed too exhausted to worry. It isn't long before I drift into a peaceful slumber.

Suddenly, I am awake, startled by breaking glass. The bright red numbers on my digital clock show it is 2:00 A.M. I hear the loud bang of a door crashing against a wall. Fatigue is swept away; I am energized by fear and my heart is pounding. Adrenaline courses through my veins as I jump up and slide my feet into the red house shoes beside my bed.

I anxiously try to reconcile the possibilities awaiting me. It can't be George. Our contact has been minimal but cordial since the divorce. I run into the hallway and flip on the light switch, illuminating the face of a young man, possibly nineteen or twenty years old, as he rushes toward me brandishing a butcher knife.

I watch in disbelief as he reaches the end of the hall and lunges at me. He hits me with enough force to knock me off my feet, then deftly catches me before I fall.

He pulls me close to him. His left arm is tightly around my waist, while he presses the sharp tip of the butcher knife's blade hard against my throat with his right hand. I know he is going to slit my throat.

My heart is throbbing in my temples, but I am beginning to regain my senses. I try to calm myself by making a mental note of his appearance. He has on a red, white, and blue muscle shirt. His hair is closely cropped to his head, like a burr or one of those military haircuts.

I feel his hand against my skin, so I know he is not wearing gloves. Although his presence is overpowering, he is not much taller than I am.

The next thought that runs through my mind is the rationalization that this stranger doesn't belong in my home. I feel my mouth open as the words tumble out, "You don't belong here!"

Pressing the point of the knife harder against my throat, he demands, "Don't scream, lady. I've got a hard dick and I'm going to fuck you!"

Now I know why he is here. I murmur, "Jesus, Jesus. God, don't let this happen to me." In a barely audible voice, I timidly ask my attacker, "Do you know Jesus?"

My question infuriates him and he responds, "No. I don't believe in God. He's let me down too many times!"

Petrified by the rage my question has created and the anger inherent in his voice, I begin to think of a way to escape.

Fear paralyzes me, but my thoughts run rampant: Is he going to kill me? How am I going to get out of this? I never thought this could happen to me. I don't want to be raped. I don't want to die.

I am overcome with panic, and my chest tightens. I am certain my lungs will explode. I realize it is imperative to remain calm and to think clearly, so I take a deep breath to steady myself.

The decision to fight to survive comes to me instinctively. With my arms, legs, and a tremendous will to live, I begin a life-and-death struggle. The attacker fights back ferociously; his determination to maintain control of me matches my will to escape.

Throughout the brief struggle, he repeats, "I'll kill you, lady, if I have to. I won't leave here 'til I get what I came after."

His strength is much greater than mine. Reluctantly, I concede the inevitable and quickly indicate with an affirmative nod of my head, saying, "I'll cooperate if you don't hurt me."

Victorious, he pushes me into the front bathroom just off the hall, directly across from Michelle's room. I don't know why, but as we enter the bathroom I reach up and quickly switch on the light.

He poses me in front of the mirror and sticks the blade of the knife under my chin, brusquely demanding, "Don't look at me, lady!" Remembering his earlier rage, and with the terrifying feeling of the knife against my throat, I avert my gaze, turning my head slightly to the right, though I continue observing him out of the corner of my left eye.

Desperate to stop the situation before it accelerates, I turn again to my faith in God, hoping to touch a place in this man's soul that will compel him to stop this horrible atrocity. With all the courage and conviction I can muster, I direct, "Satan, God didn't create this young man to commit such violent acts. I demand you flee in the name of Jesus."

As I speak, he begins to shake violently. I tremble and hold my breath in utter horror as he raises the knife high above his head, the blade pointed directly toward me.

Fearing death is imminent, I meekly ask if I can pray. Surprisingly, he grants this request. As I begin to softly pray, he brings the knife downward toward my chest, stopping just short of making contact. I think, God, he's going to kill me! He repeats this process three times, tormenting me as I shake uncontrollably and try to pray.

Abruptly, he stops. In the prevailing stillness, I manage to collect myself long enough to notice his right arm is dangling at his side and he is holding the knife limply in his right hand.

Inexplicably, he transforms from a violent persona to an apologetic little boy, saying, "I'm sorry, lady. I don't want to harm you." Maybe my prayers are working.

My thoughts turn quickly to Michelle. Her room door is only a few feet away. I cannot afford to have Michelle hear me and wake up. I pray with all my heart that my little girl is fast asleep; I know I will have to try, no matter what, to stay quiet.

His remorse, however, lasts only a moment. His rage returns with a vengeance, dispelling my hope, and he roughly pushes me into the doorknob of the bathroom, jabbing it forcefully into my back.

I suppress a scream, but the pain is excruciating and I collapse to the floor. I pretend to pass out, hoping he will find me too much trouble and leave.

I can sense his body move as he reaches toward me, then viciously jerks me to my feet. His arm is once again wrapped around my waist. He notices fresh blood is on his cheek and the white collar of his shirt, and asks, "Who's bleeding, you or me?" Looking down at himself, he hollers, "Oh, God, I've been shot! They must've shot me when I escaped from Gatesville. I'm facing a twenty-year sentence, but they won't ever catch me!"

While he carries on, I rapidly check to see if I am hurt. The index finger on my right hand had been severely slashed during the earlier struggle, and blood flows from the open laceration.

Seeking to calm and quiet him down, I hold up my finger, saying, "I'm the one who's hurt."

His demeanor becomes calmer, and he again apologizes, "Oh, lady, I'm so sorry you've been hurt. I need to bandage you." He is repelled by the sight of blood and begins frantically searching through the medicine cabinet for bandages.

I explain I have hidden the bandages in a dresser drawer because my daughter uses them on her dolls. He turns on the faucet and holds the bleeding cut under the water, declaring, "Washed in the blood of the lamb."

I am both frightened and baffled by this religious statement. I try to divert his attention back to the bandages, reminding him once more they are in the dresser. Taking me by the arm, he orders me into the bedroom and shuts the door behind us. I am in the habit of sleeping with my swag lamp on dim and beseech him not to shut the door, saying, "I'm afraid my child will wake up and miss the light from my room."

I take a step back and notice my purse sitting on the desk. It occurs to me if I offer him money he might take it and leave, but by then he too has seen my purse and curtly informs me, "I didn't come to rob you. I just came for the rape." The word hangs in the air like a vile smell. The thought of him touching me is repulsive.

He again demands I get the bandages, so I hastily reach in the drawer and pull out a plastic bag. Something makes me look up at him and ask his name. The question perplexes him, and he replies, "If I told you, you wouldn't know if I was telling the truth. Besides, I'm not gonna tell you."

He snatches the bag, yanks out some gauze and tape, then loosely wraps my finger. When he is finished, blood is still running down my hand, yet he seems satisfied with the job he's done. He grabs me by the arm and says, "Let's get on with it. I'm facing twenty years in prison, and I'm horny, so it better be good." He quietly cautions me that if my daughter wakes up and comes in, he will hurt her.

I start feeling sick all over. I believe him, but I am unable to yield my body to this man, and I resist as he tries to force me down, ordering my cooperation. The brief confrontation immediately ceases when he informs me, "You either cooperate and satisfy me, or I'll go rape and kill your little girl, and you can watch me do it!"

I am petrified. I know that Michelle's and my only chance of living through this is if I cooperate. I silently pray for the inner strength to endure the degradation to come. I know the inevitable is going to happen, and I surmise the bathroom is preferable. It is small and farther away from Michelle's bedroom, so she will be less likely to hear what is going on and awaken. I hope the cramped quarters will be so uncomfortable he will get it over with quickly.

He nods toward the bed. Observing droplets of blood on the gold thermal blanket lying across the bed, and remembering his earlier off-the-wall reaction to the blood, I request he take me into the bathroom located off the master bedroom.

To maintain as much control over the situation as possible, I turn to him, saying, "If this is inevitable, I'll have to think of it as lovemaking. No one has ever held a knife on me during love-making. I can't have the knife in my presence." I know this may seem an odd statement to make under the circumstances, but I am desperately trying to distance myself from the knife and hope this strategy will work. He places the knife in the side of his boot.

I am aware I am pushing my luck, but I persist with one last request, saying, "I don't want the knife within your reach."

"Okay, lady," he says, irritated. "But remember, I'm faster than you, and I can get to my knife a lot quicker than you can get to your kid. Try anything and you'll both be dead, understand?"

Relieved at the small victory, I nod that I understand his conditions completely. He removes the knife from his boot and places it on the floor just outside the bathroom door. I ask him to shut the door for privacy, in case my daughter awakens. He agrees.

Instead of proceeding with the attack, he becomes preoccu-pied with the blood dripping down my arm. His patchwork job hasn't been effective. My finger is still bleeding profusely, and blood is all over the floor, the vanity, and me, and he wants it gone!

He asks if I have any washcloths or towels. I indicate there are some in the hallway linen closet. We both get up, and with him closely following me, proceed to the linen closet. I open the door and reach in for a large purple bath towel and washcloth. Then he escorts me back to the master bathroom.

Seeing my gown is covered in blood, he insists I remove it. I think to myself, Oh no, here it comes. I am horrified beyond description. It embarrasses me and my face turns crimson, but I am too scared to protest exposing my body to this stranger. I remember I must do whatever I have to do to survive. Indescribable nausea knots my stomach as I take the gown off and, humiliated, drop it on the floor.

I stand nearly naked and shivering, and he orders me to wash the blood off my face. As I do this, he takes the towel and begins wiping the blood off my back. My body shudders as he reaches up and unhooks my bra, saying, "You're a very attractive woman." The bra joins my gown on the floor, and he turns me around to face him. Instinctively, I try to cover my naked breasts by crossing my arms in front of them. I cast my eyes down to avoid his. He begins taking off his clothes.

The awkward silence is broken when he removes his shirt and declares, "Look at all the scars I have on my body from all the abuse and beatings I've had to endure." Raising my eyes momentarily to examine his chest and stomach, I see nothing. I wonder if the scars he speaks of are emotional rather than physical, visible only in his mind; or if maybe he has enough presence of mind to lie about the scars so as to confuse me later when giving a physical description of him to police.

He finishes undressing and pauses long enough to ask, "How did you satisfy your husband? How long has it been since your divorce?" I do not know how to answer the questions, so I say nothing.

He begins neatly folding and stacking his shirt, pants, and underwear; his boots rest underneath the pile. He looks at me, and then demands I remove my last piece of clothing, my panties, and lie on the floor.

A disgusting feeling overpowers me. Knowing I have stalled as long as possible, I awkwardly attempt to cover myself as I, still shivering, discard the panties, and upon his instructions, place the purple towel on the floor.

Having discarded my dignity with my clothes, I am totally naked. I lie down on the towel, quickly slipping off my wedding rings, which I had continued to wear following the divorce. I push them behind the commode, along with a package of Marlboro cigarettes he had placed on the floor. I feel vulnerable, embarrassed beyond belief, humiliated, and afraid.

Eyeing my body, he asks, "You enjoy oral sex? Ever had it done to you?"

Resisting the nausea, I shudder and emphatically reply, "No!"

Straddling my chest, he jiggles his limp penis in the direction of my mouth. I am repulsed and tightly close my eyes, turn my head away and hope I will awaken any moment from this bad dream. I don't. His hips slide down lower on my body so that we are now face to face. The touch of his hand transports me back to reality, as he turns my face towards him. He bends over in an attempt to kiss me, but I manage to turn my head before his lips can touch mine. Frustrated, he shifts his attention to my ear and begins licking the outer part in a slow, circular motion, then pushes his tongue inside. My stomach heaves and I staunchly fight the urge to vomit. It is the only control I seem to have over my body.

He reaches down and I feel him insert two fingers inside my vagina, arrogantly commenting, "You like it, baby, and you know it." The nausea returns. He scoots further down my body. I cringe as he tries pushing his penis inside me. After much effort, he is still flaccid but achieves a slight penetration. After a few minutes, he complains that I am not moving around enough to please him and directs me to move my hips more. I try to move a little more to keep him from getting angry with me.

Maybe to distract him; maybe to distract myself from what is taking place; I don't know why, but I begin talking to him. I tell him I am feeling faint from losing so much blood and complain my injured finger is throbbing with pain. He seems unconcerned and continues to attempt a full penetration.

I lie there with this unfeeling, uncaring person on top of me. My thoughts are jumbled, but I know one thing: a stranger is lying naked on top of me, forcing me to have sex, as my child sleeps in a nearby room, and I don't know if she and I will make it out dead or alive!

Think, LaVonne, think!

Hoping to discourage him and conclude the attack, I say I need to use the bathroom. He lets me up and watches as I have no choice but to urinate in front of him. When I am finished, he orders me to "jack him off." I hesitate. Then I notice that look in his eyes. I comply by getting off the toilet and down on my knees before him. I hope he will climax this way and spare me the further indignity of feeling him ejaculate inside me. His penis becomes semi-erect again, and I dread it as he directs me to guide him back inside me.

Thrusting vigorously, he pushes me back against the toilet, and as he becomes harder, brags, "A man can really hurt a woman this way—you know—do some real damage!" Unprepared for the sudden brutality, I wince in pain, bite my lip, and cry out softly.

"You ever been fucked in the ass?" he asks me.

Terrified by the question, I softly whisper in an alarmed voice, "No!"

My anxiety amuses him and he taunts me, "You really want it that way, don't you, baby?"

Not waiting for a response, he changes the subject, asking if I have a boyfriend. I tell him I have been seeing two gentlemen. He stops moving, asking why such an attractive woman as myself isn't married.

The question confuses me, but I seize the opportunity to try to humanize myself to him. I begin to converse calmly, inquiring if he has a girlfriend. He asserts, "I have a girlfriend, but all women are alike. I once had a wife and two boys. So I know how you'd feel if I hurt your kid."

Having lost his erection, his penis slips out and he pulls away from me. My stomach eases when he pulls out of me. He starts masturbating his limp penis with his hand. Having achieved a partially erect penis, he instructs me to lean over the sink, so he can penetrate me from the rear. I reluctantly obey. I will obey any command...anything...I just want it over with.

Not knowing what else to do, I resume my litany of conversation, hoping to keep him calm. "Are you from Texas?" He responds with a curt, "No." I persist, "Where did you grow up?"

He answers, "Las Cruces, New Mexico." Denying the reality of my predicament, I ask his name a second time. He looks at my reflection in the mirror with a strange expression, but does not bother to respond to me.

Undaunted, I continue, "I've learned since my divorce women should be independent, not passive and dependent on men. You know, they should stand on their own two feet." Verbal vomit is spewing forth from my mouth. I just want to keep him talking, hoping he will relate to me as a fellow human being. It might save my life.

Abruptly, he stops attempting penetration from the rear and withdraws his penis, commenting, "I think your husband was crazy for leaving. You're a level-headed woman. I'll leave you alone now."

Totally surprised by his change in mood, yet not convinced the attempt at raping me is over, my fears begin to escalate that he will kill me because I have been unable to satisfy him. Picking up his clothes, he complains about the blood on them, then lays them back down.

I am scared of what will happen next. I look at my finger, and tell him I need to change the bandage because blood has soaked through. He examines my wound and recommends cold water or ice to help the bleeding stop. He reminds me of a mother telling a child how to make an injury better. Feeling trapped in the bathroom, I suggest we get some ice in the kitchen.

As we enter the dark kitchen, he thoughtfully cautions, "Watch out for the broken glass. You'll cut your feet to pieces, if you're not careful." He bends down and picks up a few broken pieces of glass and places them in the nearby trash bag. I flip on the light switch and look down. Glass covers the floor from the shattered kitchen door window, his obvious point of entry.

Since he is being kind, I think if I respond likewise, maybe he will just leave. I ask if he would like a glass of water, and he nods yes.

The fear of death haunts me, shadowing all my thoughts, and my hands shake as I carefully fill two Styrofoam cups with water. I hand him one of the cups and try to keep from spilling it. He politely thanks me, as if he were an invited guest. When he is finished with his drink, he bends down and picks up more of the pieces of broken glass, carefully placing them in the trash bag.

Once he has completed this task, he takes me back to the bathroom where he finishes dressing. I decide to take a calculated risk and ask if I can pray for him as I reach to touch his shoulder.

Furious, he says, "Don't touch me! You can pray for me, but it won't do any good. God ain't never done anything for me— ever! Don't pray 'til I'm gone, and don't call the police."

His rage disappears and he again talks calmly and kindly to me. I decide to remind him, diplomatically, that my finger will need stitches because of the deep cut.

He reflects momentarily, then comments, "I don't think you'll call the police. Just go lie down and wait thirty minutes 'til I've had time to get away. I don't want you to see which way I go. Then you can call someone to take care of your finger."

I pray harder than I have ever prayed before that he will not change his mind and kill me. He glares at me and imparts a final warning, saying, "If you go to the police, I'll find out. I'll come back and kill you and your daughter. I'll burn down your house with your dead bodies inside."

He turns to leave, but looks back at me one last time and calmly remarks, "Lady, you've hurt yourself. You need to get that finger taken care of. Just do as I say and you'll be okay."

I hold my breath until I think he is gone, then start down the hallway, staggered by what has transpired. I am naked and bleeding, wandering toward the kitchen, and am startled when the door opens. Looking into his eyes, the horrendous fear mounts. He has returned to kill me.

My heart is pounding hard and fast. I stand paralyzed as he mumbles something about getting his hat. Dumbfounded, I manage to say that he never had on a hat. Insisting he did, he pushes his way past me, heading back to the master bedroom, but stops before he reaches it, turning to ask my permission to go and retrieve it. I agree without hesitation. It is incredulous that this man who has broken into my home and violated my body should now seek permission to go into the bedroom.

He returns holding the package of Marlboro cigarettes I'd managed to push behind the toilet. Apparently, thank God, he did not see the rings. He walks past me without a word, leaving the same way he entered.

Bewildered and in shock, I meander aimlessly throughout the house and find myself standing inside my little girl's room. My child, awake and obviously frightened, asks, "Mommy, what's going on? Are you okay? Mommy, why are you bleeding? Where are your clothes?" Then, attempting to calm me down, this tiny, little girl tells me, "Don't worry, Jesus will take care of us."

I tell Michelle to go back to sleep, then walk to my room in a daze and sit down on the bed. My mind records the time on the clock. It is 3:01 A.M. All of this has transpired in just more than an hour.

I am terrified of the rapist's threats if I call the police. I pick up the phone and call my boyfriend, Brad. It seems to ring forever. Eventually I hang up and call my friend, Karen Hunter. Struggling to tell her what has transpired, I stumble through the details, lapsing intermittently into a silent daze.

Karen urges me to call the police immediately. I refuse—clinging to the belief that the attacker meant every threat he made. Determined, Karen presses me to notify the police and insists someone should be here to help me through this ordeal. Karen is certain that she should come over immediately.

Afraid to come alone, Karen decides she should call a mutual friend, Beth Adams. It is finally decided Beth's husband, Greg, a minister, will go get Karen and bring her to my house. Karen and Greg arrive at approximately 3:15 A.M.

I compose myself enough to dress while awaiting their arrival. I look in on Michelle, who has fallen back to sleep. How easy it seems to be for little children to accept things. Right now, I wish I had that ability. When Karen arrives, she comforts me and strongly counsels me to call the police. When I vigorously protest, Karen asks if she can call them.

Turning white as a sheet, I beg my friend not to intervene, saying, "No! He meant every word of his threats. He'll come back and kill us."

After considerable debate, I finally consent, and at 3:30 A.M., Karen calls the Watauga Department of Public Safety.

Within a few minutes, officers Shirley Ozuna, Bill Jackson, and David Oringderff quietly pull up in front of the house. Their unobtrusive arrival seems strange to me. I somehow expected screaming sirens and flashing lights to accompany the police.

Officer Ozuna encourages me to talk her through the scenario that took place, while the other officers systematically examine each room in which it was obvious some relevant event occurred. I tell her everything that I can recall. Later, we find out that the crime scene officers had found the glove compartment of my car open. The papers were strewn about the car.

As the crime scene officers go about their job, they offhandedly remark to me that it is very difficult to find identifiable fingerprints and they don't expect to get anything, but will dust things he might have touched anyway. I remind the officers that he had touched the broken kitchen glass window. The officers are elated when they find a perfect print on the broken glass. Other items are marked as evidence and prepared for transport to the crime lab.

As the shock begins to wear off, I try to cope with the reality of what has happened. The officers inform me that I will need to go to the hospital and submit to a rape exam and have my finger examined, and possibly stitched. Greg says he will drop Michelle off at his house and then meet everyone at the hospital.

Officer Ozuna explains to me that I will be going to John Peter Smith Hospital, a Fort Worth trauma center, specially trained to handle rape victims. As the county hospital, its staff also treats all the indigent people in the county. Everyone knows how busy it will be, and that we are all in for a long night.

The male officers remain at the house to complete their criminal investigation as Officer Ozuna, Karen, and I leave for the hospital. We arrive at 4:20 A.M.

Chapter 2

The Exam

Bedlam fills the emergency room; victims of gunshot wounds, stabbings, and accidents wander aimlessly about. I am still in a state of shock, and my predicament embarrasses me. On top of it all, I worry I will not make it to work today.

As I sit among the myriad of people, I feel conspicuous and self-conscious. Old ladies and small children are screaming. I can barely hear their loved ones strained, soothing voices above the chaos. Doctors, nurses, and orderlies are rushing around. Police gather around more victims, collecting data for their reports.

Emergency room medical personnel hustle in new arrivals. I feel estranged amid the noise and confusion. A gray-haired woman in her mid-fifties stands behind a counter assisting patients with medical insurance claims in between answering the phone. She is the only clerical person in sight, and it is obvious my wait will be a long and tedious one. It doesn't seem to matter what type of tragedy has befallen me.

Although John Peter Smith Hospital has just initiated a "Rape Awareness" program, there doesn't seem to be much awareness. I am just another number, a statistic, among the many weary and hurt people who wait for treatment. I sit here wondering if other people somehow know my shame, my embarrassment, at being a rape victim.

Officer Ozuna approaches the beleaguered gray-haired lady and inquires how much longer it will be before I am examined and my cut finger stitched up. She is told the hospital does not view a rape victim as a priority, so I do not warrant immediate attention.

However, the lady takes pity on me—for some reason—and refers me to the press conference room for some privacy. We enter the room and Officer Ozuna attempts to put me at ease by suggesting we be on a first-name basis. She tells me to call her Shirley.

It doesn't take long for Bonnie of the Tarrant County Rape Crisis Center to arrive, meet, and establish a rapport with me. Throughout this whole ordeal, Bonnie is the one bright spot in the blackest of nights. She seems to be the only one who really understands what I am going through. She is bubbly and funny, and I think she must be able to put anyone immediately at ease. I am glad she is here. Although Bonnie's attitude is uplifting, she tempers it with the respect that a rape victim requires. She is a perfect balance, and just what I need.

In 1977, Bonnie is Rape Crisis. It is a new organization and all on her shoulders.

A PayDay candy bar is brought in to help quench my growling stomach during the long wait ahead. I have elevated my slashed finger to help alleviate the bleeding, but it is still throbbing and painful. Bonnie is beginning to get really upset with the hospital personnel and quietly steps out of the room to seek medical attention for me.

Eventually, the gray-haired clerk returns with some gauze and tape to put a fresh bandage on my bloody finger. The doctor who is to stitch my finger is in surgery. It is decided that during the interim they will proceed with the rape exam.

By now it is a little past 5:00 A.M. Bonnie accompanies me into a partitioned area. Inside the small cubicle is the "rape doc" and a registered nurse. The nurse introduces everyone and briefly explains the "rape awareness" program. She indicates that both the doctor and she are specially trained to deal with the victims of rape and the trauma they suffer.

She tells me the doctor will have to ask personal and pertinent questions, and notes will be taken throughout the exam. The information is in case the attacker is apprehended and goes to trial. The nurse tells me that the doctor will leave if I become uncomfortable during the questioning. All I have to do is let them know.

I am then introduced to the "rape kit" for collecting evidence to assist the police in apprehending a suspect and in the court's trial of the defendant. The kit consists of a brochure explaining the examination process, sterile gloves, plastic swabs, slides, envelopes, plastic bags, and syringes.

The nurse asks me to disrobe and put on a hospital gown. I am freezing and silently long for a warm blanket, but I am too dazed to ask for one. She gives me plenty of time to undress before she returns and takes my blood pressure and temperature.

Next, she gives me a "morning after" pill to prevent pregnancy. The nurse tells me to follow up later by going to my gynecologist for an additional pelvic exam. All these instructions are swimming around in my head. I hope I don't forget anything.

The nurse takes notes of several bruises on my back and abrasions on different parts of my body and upper arm. She asks if I am in pain and if I can recall how the bruises got there.

I say something like, "I feel some discomfort, and I do recall being pushed into the door of my bathroom by the man who attacked me."

I am told to lie back on the examination table. I am draped for the exam. With my feet in the stirrups, I feel so vulnerable, as if the attack is being repeated. The doctor finally enters the room. I am relieved that he is gentle and kind and has a very soft voice.

After taking the necessary specimens, the doctor asks if I can tell them anything that might help the police capture the man who had attacked me. I am quiet, with little to say. However, I do manage to get out the fact that the man had penetrated me only vaginally.

My finger begins to throb again, and my lower back hurts. I am exhausted and getting extremely weak. As the doctor gently pursues the routine, he tells me he has to ask questions that may seem intrusive. He explains that all the questions are necessary to help the lab confirm my attacker's identity.

Tired, scared, and feeling very alone, I take a deep breath as the doctor asks the first question. It is followed by many more.

"Are you using any form of birth control, and if so, what kind? What was the date of your last period? Is your cycle regular? Have you ever been pregnant, and if so, what was the result (miscarriage, live birth, abortion)? If you have children, what are their ages? When did you last have intercourse prior to the assault? Are there any current problems such as a venereal disease or vaginal infections? Was the man using a condom during the attack?"

The questions fly at me, hammering in my head. Why is he asking this; why does he need to know that? These personal questions are such an intrusion, yet I know they are necessary.

Pubic hair is carefully combed from me by the nurse, who places it on microscopic slides for viewing. Three of my own pubic hairs are pulled out and packaged separately in a small envelope. Both envelopes of evidence along with the slides are sent to the lab for evaluation.

The nurse gives me a tetanus shot for the slash I suffered during the attack. I am instructed to dress and wait for Dr. Stephen Green, the surgeon. Approximately ten minutes pass before Dr. Green arrives. He gives me a local anesthetic and begins to stitch my finger.

By now it is after 7:00 A.M., and, like most victims in total denial, all I can think of is getting out of here so I won't be late to work. No matter I have had no sleep, been raped, and my finger nearly slashed off: I must get to work.

For sanity's sake, I am pretending nothing irregular, much less horrific, has occurred in my life only hours earlier. I will soon find out, not only will I not make it to work on time, I won't make it to work at all today.

I have a long and tedious day ahead of me. The lengthy police interrogation will go on for much of the day. I will not make it home until shortly after 5:00 P.M.

When I am dismissed from the hospital, Karen, Officer Ozuna, and I head for the police station. On the way, the three of us try to make small talk to ease the tension. Officer Ozuna, now "Shirley," says I am fortunate I just had my finger almost cut off, because the creep could have cut off my head. Although I understand what she is trying to say to me, the word "fortunate" is not the word I would use to characterize the night of horror I have just endured, not to mention the ordeal at the hospital and what still lies ahead.

I sigh and lean back against the car seat. I just want to go somewhere, anywhere but home, crawl in bed, and sleep. I feel so exhausted I can barely move. The small talk continues, and then the conversation turns to getting a handgun for protection. Curious, I ask, "I'm thankful I'm alive. Do you think he'll come back to hurt us, like he said he would? Would a gun be best, or maybe a big dog?"

Shirley says to do what I feel most comfortable with, but these jerks rarely come back.

The discussion soon turns to people I need to call. I specifically ask Karen not to call my parents. "I don't want to worry my folks, or anyone, with this."

I ask my companions if they understand. I notice as they exchange glances, and Karen finally says, "La Vonne, if you really don't want me to, I won't, but I think these people should know what happened." I sit silently, not responding. Shirley drops Karen by her house. The officer and I head for the Watauga Department of Public Safety.

It is approximately 7:45 A.M. when we arrive. It has been a long night and it will prove to be a long day. Sergeant Lloyd McCormick and Officer Jerry Woods are sitting inside the police station having their morning coffee. As we walk in, Dispatcher Maria Sanchez wishes us a good morning and asks if either of us would care for coffee or donuts.

I am beginning to feel the strain of it all and think perhaps a Coke might energize me more so than coffee. Sergeant McCormick goes to the icebox and hands me a Coke, and says, "Heard you had a rough night. We're gonna get him, just you wait and see."

I thank the officers for their politeness and kindness. I am then escorted to a conference table in one of the back rooms. Shirley pulls up a couple of chairs and a writing tablet, police forms, pens, and pencils.

Although it is unrealistic, I am plagued by my urge to get to work, and ask, "How long will this take?" Shirley tells me not to worry about work. She says I've been through too much of an ordeal to even think about doing anything but getting some sleep.

Shirley then asks me if I have ever been fingerprinted. Although I have been for employment purposes, all the stress and strain surges to the surface. I become furious. "Why do I need to be fingerprinted?" I ask, exasperated. "I'm the victim, not the criminal!"

Shirley notes my frustration and validates my feelings, then carefully explains that the police fingerprint experts have lifted fifty-eight prints from my home and need to rule my prints out to help in the investigation. My overreaction embarrasses me. I apologize and okay the process.

We complete the fingerprinting process, and the officers inform me that police photographs of my injuries need to be taken. We step into the back office area to afford more privacy. Photos are taken of my hand, the abrasions on my back and arm, and the knife scratch on my neck. They explain to me that all of this will be evidence in a court trial.

My "voluntary statement" is the next and perhaps most arduous of the tasks I will complete today. Because of the injury to my writing hand, Shirley volunteers to write as I speak.

For the record, I begin to relive the nightmare, describing the physical characteristics of my attacker and the terror that had taken place in what should have been the sanctity of my own home. It was an event that had only occurred hours before, but to me, well, it seems an eternity. My only desire at this moment is to go back to work and put all of this behind me.

I cannot believe the control over my life that has been wrested away from me by this man. Fear has replaced my normally peaceful state of mind. Hoping to go to work and return to normal activities seems unrealistic. I can no longer choose to forget what happened and simply go about my daily life. Choices—that seems to be the whole point. This man, in less than ninety minutes, took away my choices and my control over my life.

It is about 10:00 A.M when Karen arrives at the police station. The interrogation is in progress. She quietly pulls up a chair and sits next to me at the conference table. Shirley seems adamant that I leave out any religious references made by either myself or the attacker. She is especially adamant about me leaving out the attacker's statement, "Washed in the blood of the lamb." It is the officer's contention, if this statement comes out, that in a trial the defense might use this and construe me as some type of "religious zealot."

Although this request seems strange and unfair to me, I shrug my shoulders and acquiesce to her experience with such things. I omit the statement the attacker made while holding my bleeding finger under the faucet.

It is now close to noon and everyone wants to break for lunch and resume at 1:30 P.M. We decide to pick up some hamburgers and adjourn to the more comfortable atmosphere of Karen's home. As we walk in Karen's front door, I am startled at our reflections in the mirrored wall. But then, I am so strung out, it doesn't take much to rattle me.

Shirley notices my panic and advises me to stay calm. "It's only a wall, nothing more. No one is here but us." With nervous laughter, I apologize for my edginess.

The first thing I want to do is go into Karen's bathroom to freshen up. Once inside the bathroom, all alone with the door closed, I vividly recall the events of the previous night. My last "bath" was at the hands of the attacker as he attempted to clean the blood off me. I shudder. I look in the mirror and notice the caked, dried blood in my hair. I also notice, for the first time, spots of blood splattered on my arms.

Of course, in accordance with police procedure, I have not been allowed to bathe since the attack. This is to preserve any possible evidence linked to my attacker. I remember reading that taking a bath is the first thing most women want to do after being raped, because they feel dirty. I know it is a mistake to do this because you can wash away valuable evidence.

After a quick lunch, we drive back to the police station and the interrogation. This time Captain McDaniel joins Shirley, Karen, and me. Captain McDaniel asks if I remember what my attacker was wearing, and if he had any distinguishing scars or moles. He presses for any details that might help in the search for this man. I tell him I have no more information than I have already provided. Then I ask him about leads.

He tells me a suspect in Watauga was seen at approximately 9:00 A.M. standing in his yard. He had a small bandage on his hand from a recent cut. The captain said, "When we questioned him about the cut, he said he had cut it on a piece of broken glass.

"He also said he was leaving town today for military duty. He had a recent military-type haircut and owned a shirt as you described. The attacker was about my size, wouldn't you say? I weigh about one hundred fifty pounds, stand about five-foot-nine, except I have a small pot belly, and this guy didn't." He chuckles as he pats himself on the tummy.

I tell him I am not very good with that sort of thing, but the description seems to be pretty accurate. I tell him fear had made it difficult for me to observe much about my attacker. The captain assures me that I have been an extremely good witness and encourages me to hang in there.

The knowledge that the suspect is preparing to leave town worries me, but I feel the captain knows what he is doing. Meanwhile, I am unaware that the police department is conducting a thorough investigation and canvassing the area businesses with a description of the rape suspect. I later learn that Sergeant McCormick has questioned a local service station owner, R. A. Lindsey, who, upon hearing the description of the attacker, replied, "Hell, that sounds just like Bevers!" The sergeant then asked Mr. Lindsey if Bevers was in town. The sergeant was told Bevers purchased gas from him just the previous morning. He also stated Bevers was driving a pin-striped, bronze Ford pickup.

Out of curiosity more than anything else, I ask when the last rape had occurred in Watauga. It shocks me when Shirley tells me this is the first rape reported in five years. The captain seems to think it is not a true indicator of the crime of rape, but rather a fear on the women's part to report the crime. I thank the captain for his care and concern. He leaves to meet with lab personnel and see if anything more has turned up from the crime scene.

At 5:00 P.M., when the city employees end their workday, Shirley concludes the statement. The officer has to pick her daughter up from day care and prepare their evening meal. She says she has plenty of information and knows I am exhausted.

I have only told of two penetrations, and I feel a little strange not having competed the whole story, but I figure the officer knows what she is doing. We say our good-byes and I gather my things to go home...or somewhere. I am not sure where to go.

Chapter 3

Picking up the Pieces

In the car, en route to Karen's home, I share with her my concerns about the statement I gave the police. For one thing, the officer wouldn't let me tell about the third penetration by the attacker. Don't they need that information to be completely accurate? Further, I express my concern about leaving out the attacker's statement: "Washed in the blood of the lamb." After all, the attacker said it, not I.

Karen tells me not to concern myself with these worries, to just trust in the Lord and leave it with Him. Then she says, on an upbeat note, "Now, let's get you cleaned up and into something more comfortable. Would it bother you to stop by your house and pick up some clothes?"

My heart starts pounding hard against my chest. I adamantly declare, "I don't want to go back to that house, ever!" Then I find myself pathetically pleading with her. "Can we just go to your place and let me borrow a house dress, please?"

Little did I know just how unrealistic this statement would prove. Here I am, a single working mother with a five-year-old daughter to support. The divorce had yielded me little but the precious equity I have in my home. I can't leave—can't afford that luxury. I am destined to be in that house for a long time. But for the moment it not only seems realistic; it seems necessary.

My understanding friend, bless her heart, says it is okay. She will take care of me. "Hey, no problem. You are welcome to stay the weekend at my house. My mom can keep the boys." I am just beginning to receive the overwhelming outpouring of love, support, and concern from my friends. Through this I will learn how wonderful my friends, and later, even George, my ex, are to me.

At her house, Karen lets it out that she had told my parents. This troubles me. Both my parents have heart problems, and I constantly worry over their health. I am never concerned about their unwavering support and love. I just do not want them to be additional victims of the rapist. Then she says that my boss and coworkers are aware of my situation as well. Further humiliation cloaks me, although I don't quite know why.

Intellectually, I understand I have done nothing wrong. Emotionally, I have not come to terms with all that has happened. This is not only a crime, but in the 1970s people are not enlightened about the nature of the crime of rape. No one wants to talk about it. Rape has a sexual connotation to it. It will be decades before it is known as a power trip for the rapist, and before people will know how to react to the victim. In any event, I am disturbed and embarrassed to know I will have to face my colleagues, and that they know my body has been violated. The rapist's reach is much further than I'd ever imagined. He isn't even here, and he is still able to degrade, humiliate, and embarrass me. I wish the whole thing would go away.

I fall asleep for a short nap in Karen's armchair. She awakens me and offers me a chance to freshen up with a warm washcloth and towel. She also offers me a house dress hanging on the hanger behind the bathroom door.

She tells me that a mutual friend of ours, Carla, has called from the singles class at church and is coming over shortly. This is how I find out the class has been told what has happened to me and is praying for me. Carla will contact Don, Hugh, Brad, Rufus, Brenda, and Donna to come over to see me, if I feel up to it.

George also calls to say Michelle is staying the weekend with my parents. I know everything is being done to comfort me, but I can't help feeling more intrusion in my life with each new person who is allowed a glimpse of this extremely personal crisis.

I thank Karen for being a good friend and proceed to take a sponge bath. Then I tell her I need to lie down for awhile. It is now a quarter past six in the evening. Karen sings out as cheerfully as she can muster, "La Vonne! Carla and Rufus are here! Do you feel like having some company?"

I wander sleepily into the den to join the others. I thank them all for their concern and support and express my good fortune at having such good friends. Karen offers food to the company. She mentions to Rufus that I need to get some clothes to spend the weekend, but she fears going alone into the house to get them. Rufus agrees to accompany her.

Carla and I sit in the living room and continue to talk quietly after Karen and Rufus have left. The doorbell rings. I jump. Carla looks out the front living room window. Don is parking his red Corvette. Brad is at the door.

"Where's La Vonne?" asks Brad. "We came over as soon as we could."

Don, a court reporter, complains that he's been in court all day and says he will be doing transcripts all Saturday and Sunday, even missing church.

He quickly adds, "Brad and I thought we'd stay over tonight and tomorrow night. Hugh also said he could stay. There should be plenty of us guys around to make you feel safe."

Poor Don. He doesn't realize the fifth infantry wouldn't be able to give me the peace of mind I long for tonight. In fact, it will escape my grasp for the next sixteen years.

Brad hurries in to see me in the den. "Hey, look at my girl! Can't leave you for one evening without all hell breaking loose."

I jump up and run to him, reaching up and putting my arms around him. He lifts me off the floor and crushes me to him, and he says, "I'll never let you out of my sight ever again." I am so glad to see Brad. I instantly forgive Carla for calling him. We barely sit down before a car horn honks. Karen and Rufus are back; Brenda and Donna pull up behind them. The gang is all here. Rufus carries my overnight bag into the house with Karen, Brenda, and Donna trailing close behind.

I am touched, although nonplussed, when my ex, George, comes to see me. We have a prayer meeting, followed by lively conversation as everyone attempts to keep my mind off what has happened. Rufus gently kisses me on the cheek and says, "Gotta go, kid." Carla and Donna walk Rufus to the door, and Karen thanks him for coming.

Karen sees that I am getting extremely tired and notices the blood still in my hair. She offers to give me a shampoo. I thank her but decline. I am so tired I just want a hot bath and some sleep. After I take the much-longed-for warm bath, Karen shows me to my room, and I lie down as Karen rejoins the others.

I can hear wafts of friendly laughter and conversation coming from the other room, and I lie in bed feeling warm and safe until I begin to think of all the events that have taken place in the last twenty-four hours. The vivid memories and the dark room make me feel isolated from the world. Memories of the earlier terror wash over me, and the rapist's face begins to take on satanic proportions in my mind.

I glance wildly around in the dark, seeing nothing but sensing a presence at every window in the room. I can picture the rapist's piercing eyes staring back at me, warning me not to tell! His eyes glare at me from every window. Panic seizes me, and my heart begins to pound so hard I think it may explode. Sweat dampens my hands.

Finally, I muster the courage to get up and run down the long hallway toward the den to my friends. "La Vonne! What are you doing out of bed? We thought you were resting. Were we too loud? Did we wake you?" asks Karen.

"Yes, I'm tired, but I don't want to be left alone right now. Sorry, I'm just not myself. It sounds so much more interesting in here," I lie.

"La Vonne, I really think you should get some rest," Karen insists. She turns and addresses the others. "Guys, she has had a rough day. Help me convince her to go back to bed."

"Karen, I think we all should turn in. Perhaps it'd be better if everyone got some rest," says Brad. "Are we all agreed?"

"That's a good idea," Don interjects. "We really have served our purpose, and we need to let these ladies get their rest." Brenda and Donna look at one another, nod in agreement, and head for the door. Hugh walks them to their car.

Saturday we spend the day wondering what the police are doing, but the day comes and goes uneventfully. I keep praying they will soon catch my attacker. The singles class shows up again for their "La Vonne Watch."

Early on Sunday, around 7:00 A.M., Millie Haney, from my singles class, calls me to express her sorrow at what had happened. She asks about my living arrangements to ensure that I will not be alone, and offers to have me stay with her a couple of nights.

The rapist's far-reaching hand is still getting to me. I no longer feel like an adult, but like a child who is scared of the bogeyman.

I stop thinking about myself and focus on Karen. She has her two sons to consider. I need to start thinking about other accommodations. I am grateful for Millie's generous offer. She has the ability to offer a friendly hand or ear and not seem intrusive.

After church Sunday evening, Brad tells me that he feels we need to talk about what happened. He says he really loves me, but feels he has been in denial. "I love you, baby. I know you need to talk about this. It concerns me this could affect the rest of our lives." He tells me that this will be the last time he ever wants to bring up the matter.

I sit on Brad's lap, recounting my nightmare. I end my story, and Brad begins his rampage, saying, "Baby, if I'd been there, this never would have happened. I would have killed that son-of-a-bitch! I'm angry I had no control over what happened to you. They should never have abolished the death penalty for rapists." That moment places a strain on our relationship.

I will learn that the crime of rape leaves no relationship untouched. It either strengthens it or destroys it; mine is no exception. Like so many other men, Brad is most angry at himself and his inability to be in control over the real issue. After the attack, Brad begins spending more time with Karen and less with me. My heart breaks. I can see the signs. I am about to lose a boyfriend and what I thought was a dear friend. The rapist just keeps taking and taking, maintaining control over my life. I wonder if I will ever get any measure of control back.

Tonight, after Brad makes me tell him about the attack, he drives me back to Karen's. Karen's children will be returning, and I know I need to leave. I make arrangements with Millie.

On Monday, Karen drops me off at work. It is June 27, my first day back after what seems like a lifetime. Everything appears smooth, and Dr. Ross Harvel and my coworkers seem genuinely happy to have me back. Although I think working will help occupy my mind, I find it difficult to concentrate.

It concerns me that I have heard nothing from the police. I call Bonnie at Rape Crisis to see if she has heard anything. Bonnie has been told that the police are working on a suspect's identification. When they have a strong suspect, I will either view a line-up or mug shots to see if I can identify my attacker.

But bad news continues to haunt me.

After lunch, Dr. Harvel asks to speak to me. For no apparent reason, I have butterflies dancing in my stomach. As a result of cutbacks mandated by the school financial bill, Dr. Harvel is afraid I may be let go. After all, I have less seniority than anyone else. He assures me in our meeting that this has absolutely nothing to do with the rape. It is merely bad timing. Nevertheless, I am facing another blow. Being a single mom without a job is devastating.

Millie picks me up from work and heads to her home just off Glenside Drive in Fort Worth. Her home is neat and set back from the main road. While Millie changes clothes, I speak briefly with my parents and Michelle. My parents assure me that Michelle is all right, despite her frightening ordeal and missing her mommy. I tell my mom that I never want to see that house again.

"At some point in time, La Vonne, you'll have to come to terms with all of this. The house is just a house. It's not the villain."

Millie overhears this conversation, and volunteers to let me stay with her. "Look, you keep me company, and I'll keep you safe. When we grow tired of each other, you can decide what to do next."

The rapist has reduced my control to the point that I require others to take care of me. I still am on the phone with my mother, and I ask to speak to Michelle, who seems happy and unscathed by our ordeal. She loves being with her grand-parents and the excitement that goes with a change.

The next day at work, when Dr. Harvel telephones and says he needs to meet with me, that feeling of doom and gloom comes over me again. He has received word on the Governor's decision regarding the school finance bill, and the news is not good. As kind and gentle as Dr. Harvel is in giving me the news, he cannot soften the blow.

The bottom line: I am out of a job, just a few days after the rape. I can see the sadness in Dr. Harvel's eyes; he tells me he'll be happy to write a letter of recommendation and try to help me find a new job. Dr. Harvel and his wife, Lil, have always been good, decent people, and I know it hurts him deeply to have to be the bearer of such sad news on top of everything else I have endured. I thank him for his kindness and appreciation, and for delivering the message personally.

The sadness I feel in my heart mixes with trepidation. I will no longer be surrounded by my coworkers, who are more like family. And I will have the additional strain of looking for a job. I can't afford to be out of work for very long.

Millie pulls up in her baby-blue Pinto to take me home. "Well, it will never be the same. There aren't many jobs where coworkers are also dear friends," I say, giving her the latest news. I blink back my tears and try to swallow the knot that has formed in my throat. Millie empathizes with my situation. She is frustrated she can't change it.

It is late. Tonight is no different than any other since the rape. Millie is asleep. Nighttime is not a comfortable experience anymore. I don't look forward to the setting sun. I crawl into bed and turn out the lights, but sleep is not near, and the glow of the night light provides little comfort.

The loud rattling of the doorknob startles me from my sleep. Oh, my God! Someone is trying to force his way into Millie's home! I sit upright in bed, covering my mouth with both my hands to stifle the screams fighting to get out.

Millie reaches into a drawer at her bedside and pulls out a gun. As she does so, she leans over the side of the bed and picks up the telephone. Holding it between her legs as she sits on the side of the bed, she tries to gain a modicum of composure. I am terrified and start to whimper.

"Shhh! He will hear you. I have my gun ready. I'll shoot through the door, if I have to!" exclaims Millie. The shadow forms a silhouette of a man holding a weapon, which we can clearly see through the window shade covering the glass door.

Millie frantically, but quietly, dials the police. I sit frozen in fear staring at the mysterious silhouetted figure. Could it be my attacker? How could he have found me at Millie's? Had he been watching my every move? I can't believe this is happening again.

An officer answers Millie's call, saying, "Fort Worth Police Department, Sergeant Swinson."

"This is Millie Haney. I'm at 3848 Nellora Avenue in Fort Worth. Got that? I'm whispering so the prowler won't hear me. He is at my bungalow door. My friend, La Vonne, is here with me. She was raped in Watauga a few days ago. I don't know if this is the same guy or not, but we're scared to death. Send a police car! We think he's got a gun and is trying to break in.

God, he's still rattling the door! Help us, please!" pleads Millie in a hoarse whisper into the phone.

"Take it easy, ma'am. We're dispatching a squad car now. It will take ten to fifteen minutes for an officer to respond. Most of our officers are tied up and it's really busy. Just stay on the phone with me," orders the sergeant.

Millie responds, "Fifteen minutes! We could be dead by then! I'm about to shoot through the door with my gun! Do you hear me?"

"Hang in there, ma'am. We'll get someone there ASAP. Meantime, if he does break in—shoot to kill!" orders the sergeant.

In approximately twelve minutes, the police arrive. But, to us, it seems like an hour. At some point, the man crept away, leaving the two of us frozen in terror. Although Millie is distraught, she still has the gun trained on the door.

I am wondering, Was it him? Will he come back? I can't handle living in fear anymore.

"They're here. Thank God!" Millie tells the sergeant on the phone.

"Good. The officers should be approaching the house together. They will knock on the door and announce themselves. Don't shoot! Let me know when you hear them at the door," warns the sergeant.

Shortly, there is a rap at the door, followed by the declaration, "Police officer, don't shoot! Everything is under control."

Millie tells the sergeant the officers have arrived, and the sergeant warns her not to hang up yet. He wants her to look outside and be certain it is the police. Millie sighs, puts her gun down, and peeks out. She sees two Fort Worth Police officers. She lets them in.

"Hello, I'm Millie Haney, and this is La Vonne Skalias. Did you see him?"

I jump in. "He has us scared to death. He kept turning the doorknob and shaking it, for what seemed like forever. You are a welcome sight."

Millie turns her attention back to the phone. "Sergeant? The officers are inside. Thank you very much." They bid each other goodnight. The police officers complete their report and leave. Millie and I are both visibly shaken, but we eventually manage to fall asleep. That night the rapist returns to invade my sleep in the form of nightmares.

My last two days at work are sad. I bid farewell to my extended family. I stay a few more days with Millie. Millie is a good friend and I don't want to impose on that friendship, but more than that, I don't want Millie caught in the middle if my attacker is stalking me. This is my nightmare; I am not about to drag anyone else into it.

I express to Millie my fear that the prowler might return, endangering her life, but Millie confidently assures me that God and her "Saturday Night Special" will protect us. A good combination, I think to myself. After deliberation, I call my Aunt Ann and Uncle Tony to baby-sit me next.

After he hears about the prowler, my uncle warns me not to discuss my whereabouts with anyone. "You never know who's involved in this thing."

My aunt is happy to see me, and tells me with a slight giggle that my parents are a little worse for the wear, trying to keep up with a five-year-old at their age. She hopes that I will be able to get back to my normal routine and return home with Michelle. "The police are on top of this thing. You'll be safe now."

However, my strongly opinionated uncle cuts her off. "Nah, Ann, you're telling her wrong. Police don't do a damn thing anymore! Laws tie their hands. People in Austin are too busy linin' their pockets with people's hard-earned money. We're being too damn lenient on these criminals today! La Vonne, you stay with us and bring Michelle over here, too, if you need to. Ya hear?"

My Uncle Tony is quite a character. He played major league baseball in 1935. When he finally hung up his glove, he left the field, but not the sport. He became a scout, and was responsible for signing players. He knew many baseball greats, from Babe Ruth to Mickey Mantle. On a flight back to D/FW, he met (former) Dallas Cowboys quarterback Roger Staubach, and they talked sports. Uncle Tony compared his World Series ring with Staubach's Super Bowl ring. He declared that Roger's ring won hands down! Uncle Tony is a man's man who believes in speaking his mind. He isn't about to stop now.

I sleep well in the big four-poster bed my first night in their home, knowing my uncle is near. The lamp stays on all night, sending a warm red glow over the room. It is a nice feeling being with my family and feeling safe. It's a feeling that won't last long.

By the second night, visions of the rapist creep into my mind. Nervous and agitated, I toss and turn before finally falling into a fitful sleep. Sometime during this restless sleep I cry out,

"Get out! Leave me alone…I'll kill you!" Now, awake and sobbing, I ask myself, Oh God, will he ever leave me alone?

My screams awake my aunt and uncle, who rush into the room. "You okay, honey? We could hear you all the way in our room. You gotta get a grip on yourself, honey" my uncle implores.

"I'm sorry. I must have had another nightmare. He even haunts me in my dreams. I can't escape him. He won't get out of my head! I'm sorry I woke y'all. I'm all right now."

Everyone returns to bed. I stay with my aunt and uncle until Friday morning. They try to talk me into staying longer. I thank them, but ask if they'll drive me over to my parent's house. I have decided to take mom up on her offer to stay with her and dad. I feel safe and sound, once again a child protected by her parents.

Days pass and I realize that the rapist not only took away my dignity, he took away the most precious commodity for an adult—independence. Being an only child, I had the good fortune of having my parents' undivided attention. I reminisced about playing with dolls instead of a brother or sister. I had the luxury of being afforded piano, organ, tap, tumbling, and ballet lessons.

My family has always been active in church. Larry Gatlin and his famed brothers used to sing in our church, and I was amazed as I watched Larry change from a freckled-face little boy into a handsome country star. Listening to Larry's music helped me during my separation and divorce from George, with lyrics such as, "She's a broken lady, waiting to be mended" playing on my stereo and speaking to my heart. Oh, how the memories flood back.

My mom abruptly interrupts my thoughts when she hollers that I have a phone call. "George wants to talk to you." I am in what has become my usual state of confusion. I wonder... did Mom say George was on the phone? It had really taken me by surprise when he came over to Karen's shortly after the rape to check on me. We've had little contact since our divorce, and I hadn't expected to hear from him again after that brief visit.

Curious, I pick up the phone. "George? What time is it? What day is it?"

"It's 7:30, Saturday morning, July 2," George replies. "I've made some arrangements for you guys, and I won't take no for an answer," he emphasizes in his heavy New York accent. He goes on to tell me he has three round-trip tickets to New York to see his family. "I still care about you and Michelle. I want you safe, and that creep's not been caught. No strings attached, I promise."

I can't imagine where this new attitude of George's is coming from. He has been negligent in paying child support, and the divorce, caused by irreconcilable differences, had left us both bitter. Now this same man is showing compassion I haven't seen in a long time. My knees are suddenly weak, and I sink into the nearest chair. Things are happening too fast. My mind isn't functioning well. I struggle to answer him. I have to think this thing out.

"La Vonne, baby doll, you there?" George's voice over the phone forces me back into the moment.

I blurt out, "Yes, George, I'll go with you. I don't know why, but I will. Lately I don't know what's best for Michelle, or me. Right now I need to lean on and trust you. Can I do that for a little while?" I ask, aware I sound doubtful.

"What kind of a question is that? You know you can. I just feel so bad this happened to you, and Michelle being there to hear it all. It makes me angry enough to want to kill this guy. The best I can do is get you two away for awhile—a diversion for a few days." He goes on to say I shouldn't rush back home; that I need more time to adjust. He tells me he will meet me at the house and help me pack. "I promise you won't have to go in there alone. We'll get it done, okay?"

"Okay, all right," I mumble.

"That's my girl! Now, get going. We leave D/FW Airport at 12:35 today, so we've got to move. My brother Russ will pick us up. The whole gang will be there except Uncle Hal, so hurry." I ask what's up with Uncle Hal, and George says he is working for the Port Authority at JFK Airport and something heavy is going on, but that we will see him eventually.

No doubt about it, when he wants to be, George can be charming. He meets me at the scene of the crime to pack.

Entering the house sends cold chills down my spine. The house looks the same as it did before the rape, but it doesn't feel the same! I scream. Was there a man holding a knife? No, just ghosts all around me...would he ever stop haunting me? I am visibly shaken and trembling all over.

I am frozen just inside the door. The sound of George's voice asking me what the matter is brings me out of my nightmare. I take a deep breath to calm down; I secretly wish I knew when these flashbacks will stop. The truth is, they may never stop. As I gather my belongings for the trip, I can feel the rapist's presence in every room. Memories flood back from that terrible night.

While I am packing there is a knock at the door. George answers it. A small, frail woman, in her late forties or early fifties, greets him in a dignified voice. With her long straight hair and large blue eyes, she resembles a hippie time has forgotten.

The woman seems anxious to tell us something about the attack. She tells George she thinks she knows who raped me. I walk up beside George, trying to remain calm, and say, "Hello. You say you know who attacked me?"

"Hi, I'm Aggie Wallace. I live two doors down. I think the man that raped you is the same man I chased out of my backyard early last Friday morning with a shotgun. My collies were barking up a storm. I woke up around 1:45 in the morning. I crawled down the hall on my hands and knees and saw him at my patio door. I saw him trying to get in, and I took my shotgun from the table top. It was empty, but I decided to bluff my way. I shoved the gun at him and hollered, 'You son-of-a-bitch, get off my property before I kill you. You've no business here. Get going, or I'll kill you.' He fled over my backyard fence and jumped the next fence into your backyard. After that, I lost sight of him."

I study her carefully. The first thought that crosses my mind, strange as it might seem, is that this woman might be the rapist's mother trying to see if I know anything. But Aggie comes across as frightened and concerned.

Then I consider: Guilt could be a key to her emotions. It makes sense that she may be feeling some guilt, because when I ask Aggie if she called the police that night and reported a prowler, Aggie tells me she didn't.

"I didn't report it. I'm petrified of him. I've seen him before standing out by the back fence smoking cigarettes. I'm the mother of two boys. This boy has a mother. I couldn't bring myself to turn him in. Please understand. I'm just scared to death of him."

Her remarks astound me. I think how strange people are sometimes. How could her having two boys be a defense for not turning this prowler in? I have heard before that some women jurors with boys refuse to convict on rape cases because they just can't bring themselves to convict a boy of this crime. It is truly difficult to understand human nature.

My demeanor changes with lightning speed. I practically yell, "You didn't call the police? What the hell were you thinking? He could have broken into your house, and you would have been in my position."

George interjects, "Worse yet, you could both be dead at the hands of this maniac."

"I'm sorry you feel that way. I didn't expect you to understand a lonely woman scared for her life. I've said enough. I'm really sorry for what's happened to you. I doubt he'll ever come back. He knows the police are looking for him. Be careful, and get a gun, if you don't have one." On that note, the mysterious lady turns, and abruptly as she arrived, leaves.

George and I watch her as she walks the two houses down to where she lives. "Wow! Can you believe her? She didn't even report this to the police," George says.

Strangely enough, I can understand. This guy does give you the creeps. He has the ability to make you believe you're dead if you go to the police. I do the only thing I can and shrug it off. I finish packing quickly. I want to get out of this house!

George, Michelle, and I board the plane bound for New

York. As the plane touches down at JFK Airport, Michelle cries out with glee, "Hello, New York! I can't wait to see Grandma." Michelle runs ahead of her father and me through the airport. We are walking as fast as possible to keep up with her, but she remains in the lead.

We hear Grandma Skalias cry out, "Hello, everybody!" It has been about four years since I last saw my ex-mother-in-law and the rest of the Skalias family. The divorce has not changed our feelings toward each other. We are still family. As I had been informed earlier, Uncle Hal is noticeably missing from the group.

Out of curiosity, more than anything, I approach his wife, Aunt Valerie, and ask if Uncle Hal is still at work. "Yes, Hal is always working late. We have so many things going on. Police work never seems to go away," she responds.

Aunt Valerie goes on to explain Uncle Hal is working the now infamous Son of Sam murders. She explains to me that the murderer's first victim, Donna Larient, was a friend and neighbor of Grandma Skalias. She says Donna and her fiancé, Johnny, were parked just outside Donna's house when they were shot. Donna died and Johnny was permanently blinded.

Cousin Paula pipes in, "Yeah, Dad wants Mom to wear her hair up, because most of the women victims had long brown hair."

"No way," interrupts Aunt Valerie. "I'm not gonna wear my hair up because of some creep. He's not going to control me!"

Bingo, I think. That's the whole issue of terrorists—control!

On the subway, I see a young man who looks like my attacker. I muster the nerve to stare him down, and he flees the subway car, pushing his way through the crowd. I know I'll never forget the attacker's face. It is embedded forever in my memory.

Our time in New York passes quickly. For the first time I am able to think about something other than the attack, but it is never completely out of my mind.

On Sunday, July 10, the three of us bid farewell to all the relatives. On the flight home, I think about the impact of what happened to me that fateful night back home. This stranger has stolen my dignity and punished me with physical and mental pain. He terrorized me, robbing me of my pride and stealing my independence. No matter where I am, whether at work, church or New York, my mind drifts off, as though in a trance, because of this one man. That is what he stole most of all: my peace of mind.

I silently wonder if the police have made an arrest in my absence. Knowing this is a possibility, I dread having to see this man in a line-up. It seems he will forever entwine his life with mine.

I am apprehensive about having to go back to my house. Despite everyone else's assurances, I know it could be dangerous should he return to carry out his threats. No one really takes my attacker's threats to return seriously, except me. The way he threatened me after the rape made me believe him. Some people suggest if I am so worried he may come back, for my peace of mind, I should move. But they don't know how financially strapped I am. Moving will have to wait.

Chapter 4

The Investigation

The rapist remains free. The week drags on. There is no word from Bonnie at Rape Crisis or the police. I know they will catch him, but I am resigned to it taking a long time. My thoughts keep returning to how he threatened me. How he said he would kill me...kill my daughter. And, he is out there somewhere...free.

I am on the receiving end of a lot of free advice, proving once again that talk is cheap. I know people mean well, but no one wants to deal with the reality of this type of crime—the one that happens to someone else, never to them. The majority of people are content to live in a bubble, only facing this kind of ugly reality when they become a statistic.

Becoming a victim often acts as a catalyst for those affected to try to change the system. After I was raped, a friend stated, "La Vonne, there are plenty of victims to change our system." Later, I wondered why she stayed in the background and didn't take a stronger stance to fight crime.

It seems an eternity before I hear from the police. Finally, on Monday, July 18, Officer Shirley Ozuna calls me. She excitedly tells me that Captain McDaniel and Officer McCormick would like to come by either Tuesday or Wednesday. She asks which day is best for me.

I briefly consider my situation. I have been going to job interviews, but without any results. I do not have any interviews Wednesday, so we make an appointment for 10:00 A.M., Wednesday, July 20.

It has been twenty-six days since the attack. Shirley will not confirm the nature of the appointment, and I do not press her. She does indicate it is in-line with the police department's routine procedure.

I call my mom. As I start telling her what is happening, I begin pacing and become audibly nervous. "Mom, I wish I knew what they're doing. He should've been arrested by now. I'm afraid he's left town." Mom offers me the reassurance I need from her, and I begin to calm down, although I continue to ponder nervously what the visit will be about long after I've hung up the phone.

Is there going to be a police lineup or just more questioning? During our trip to New York, George offered me some sound advice about viewing a photo lineup. He said to cover up the hair and just look at the facial features. His reasoning was that guys can disguise themselves by the length or color of their hair, so concentrating on the face makes the most sense.

Wednesday arrives, and although I am expecting the officers, the doorbell startles me. I think, Everything startles me these days. I run to answer it; my heart is fluttering. I open the door and invite Captain McDaniel and Sergeant McCormick into the living room.

Captain McDaniel begins the conversation. "First off, Mrs. Skalias, I'd like to have you walk us through the scenario that occurred on June 24, just to refresh our minds on what actually happened, best as you can recall." Obliging the two officers, I reenact the horrible events that happened that night. Reliving the episode exhausts me, and I sit down at the kitchen table with the officers.

Sergeant McCormick speaks softly. "Mrs. Skalias, please take your time and don't feel you have to rush. We're in no hurry. Carefully study each face," he says as he lays down pictures of several different men on the kitchen table. "We expect to arrest the proper individual, once we have your identification."

Captain McDaniel adds, "There are seven photographs for you to carefully observe. Good luck to you." I am scared. Scared he will not be in the photographs. Then, alternately scared he will be there, staring back at me. I take a deep breath, try to relax, and consider George's advice. With my fingers, I cover the hairlines of each individual in the photographs.

Very carefully I study their features. I spot the attacker and cry out without hesitation or doubt, "That's him! He's here, thank God!" Captain McDaniel asks if I am absolutely positive of the identification. I enthusiastically respond that I am positive.

"Good girl!" exclaims Captain McDaniel, then he adds, "Be prepared for this to take a long time. The wheels of justice turn very slowly, Mrs. Skalias. Hang tough. We'll get him. The arrest warrant will be issued just as soon as we get everything nailed down."

I am geared up and anxious to get the show on the road and over. I wait patiently. Yet time seems to drag. I learn the attacker's name is Lanny Gene Bevers, Jr. He attacked me the night before the military shipped him to Germany. I learn it will take a lengthy paper trail and extradition to return Bevers to the states. Once he is back, he will be held in the stockade at Fort Bragg, North Carolina. From there the military will transfer him to Tarrant County, where he will be placed in a cell in the Tarrant County Jail to await trial.

I did not expect such a long, arduous ordeal in getting the attacker into a Tarrant County jail. Of course, after putting two and two together, I realize why my attacker's hair was so short...he is a serviceman! All in all, it will take eight months to extradite Bevers back to Tarrant County, Texas, to await trial.

I didn't know it would take several more months just to get things under way after he arrived in Tarrant County.

It is early August, when Bonnie at Rape Crisis contacts me to suggest I take a lie detector test. The inference makes me angry. "What kind of stupid idea is that? I'm telling the truth. Why should I have to take a lie detector test?" Not giving her a chance to answer, I indignantly continue, "Isn't it enough I've been subjected to being fingerprinted like a common criminal? Now they want me to take a lie detector test. Who's the nit-wit that thought this one up?" Her response takes me by surprise.

"You're talking to her, dear. I'm the nit-wit. I know it doesn't make sense to you, but it is necessary. Rape's a difficult crime to prove. Any cooperation you can give to the police and to the process of the law to get this guy to trial will be well worth the effort. Trust me, La Vonne, I've been there. I understand. It's for your own good. Besides, you don't have anything to worry about. When they bring Bevers back here, he'll be in custody of Tarrant County, and we will see to it that he gets a lie detector test, if it's within the boundaries of the law. It will look bad for him should he decline a test, since you so openly stepped forward to take one."

Bonnie goes on to explain to me that she has secured an appointment with Major Gilbert at the Hurst Police Department and wants to know if I can be ready by 1:30 P.M. today. I tell her I trust her and will be ready to go, but my heart isn't in it. The morning lingers on. Finally, it is time for the appointment. I am introduced to Major Gilbert. He seems to be a patient man. He tries to put me at ease and takes the time to explain the procedure carefully.

The machine doesn't look so complex. There is "chart paper" that feeds through the machine. A needle tracks my reaction to each question and records the results by sweeping back and forth on the paper.

Sitting in the school desk chair with the right wooden arm curved outward, I nervously rest my right arm on the curved portion of the desk. Gilbert's assistant hooks me to the machine. Wires run from the machine and to the fingers of my right hand. These will measure my pulse rate. Two large, black bands stretch across my chest, to measure my breathing. The machine will detect any change in my reaction to the questions via the measuring devices.

"La Vonne," Gilbert explains, "these questions will be simple to understand. Relax and answer each question truthfully with only a 'yes' or 'no.' There will be ten basic questions, and some of those will be repetitious. Take your time when responding to each question. If you do not understand the question, I will repeat it. Do not talk. Again, answer only 'yes' or 'no.'"

I repeat, "You'll repeat the question if I remain silent, but I am not to tell you if I don't understand the question, right?"

"That's right," he says, "just remain silent and I'll repeat the question. These are simple questions and to the point. You will know how to respond to them. Shall we begin?"

"Okay," I say.

"La Vonne, we are beginning the exam. Please answer the following questions with a 'yes' or 'no' response only."

"Are you Nancy La Vonne Skalias?"

"Yes."

"Do you live at 1922 Presley Drive?"

"Yes."

"Are you Nancy La Vonne Skalias?"

"Yes."

"Are you a resident of Tarrant County, Texas?"

"Yes."

"Do you know the man who raped you?"

"No."

"Do you live at 1922 Presley Drive in Watauga?"

"Yes."

"Were you raped?"

"Yes."

"Are you Nancy LaVonne Skalias?"

"Yes."

"Did you identify a picture of the man who raped you?"

"Yes."

"Do you have a daughter named Michelle?"

"Yes."

"Were you raped?"

"Yes."

"Do you live in Watauga, Texas?"

"Yes."

"Were you raped, LaVonne?"

"Yes."

"Are you a resident of Tarrant County, Texas?"

"Yes."

"Did the man that raped you ejaculate?"

"No."

"Did the man that raped you climax?"

"No."

"Are you Nancy LaVonne Skalias?"

"Yes."

Gilbert explains to me that the test is now over and to just relax. He tells me it shouldn't take long for his assistant to unhook me from this contraption. I politely thank him and breathe a quiet sigh of relief.

Before he walks away, Gilbert inquires, almost offhandedly, "Off the record, I'd like to ask you a perplexing question. Why didn't he climax after penetrating you vaginally? The lab didn't find any semen. He should have reached a climax. I've never understood this in all the twenty-two years I've been a cop. It seems that most rapists I've run across reach a climax, but this one didn't. How would you respond to that?".

Offended and confused at his question, I reply, "I don't know anything about rapists. I just know that I was raped. I know he didn't ejaculate. You ask me why…I don't know."

Although Gilbert is a knowledgeable person with plenty of street smarts, his observation is not unlike the majority of the public who know little about the motives of rapists. Later, I learn power and control are their climaxes, not sex.

As he turns to walk away, he says, "Well, La Vonne, we will analyze everything and give you the results shortly. You can wait in the outer office, if you wish. It may be a little more comfortable for you. Just sit tight, and I'll be back before you know it."

As he tears off the chart paper, I take off down the hall. For some reason, I think he didn't believe me. I cannot understand the questions about the attacker climaxing. I stop by the water fountain for a drink. The test has left my mouth dry. Probably nerves. I head back down the hall. I begin to feel uncomfortable.

In only a few minutes, Gilbert appears in the doorway.

"You've passed with flying colors. Congratulations, La Vonne, for a job well done!" commends Gilbert. His attitude toward me seems to have changed after he got his results. That makes me feel much better.

On my way out, I pause and ask the police chief's secretary if they have any job openings. I explain I have been laid off and need full-time employment. I am told to check with City Hall in the personnel department.

I go directly to City Hall and fill out an application. I take a typing test at the Texas Employment Commission and apply for a position in the Engineering Department of the City of Hurst.

I continue to search for a job and finally secure one with a company. Two weeks later, the city offers me a job. I immediately quit and go to work for the city. Finally, good things are beginning to happen. I am hoping my luck is changing.

In late August, Bonnie calls me. "Well, I have some news, but nothing you really want to hear," she warns. Feeling any news is better than no news, I implore her to go on and tell me. Bonnie begins an incredible story, saying, "It seems the photographs you identified are missing. Have you been keeping up with the newspapers?"

My curiosity peaks. I answer, "No."

Bonnie takes a deep breath (as if to steady herself) and forges ahead. "Captain McDaniel has been arrested on charges of burglary. He is accused of going into people's homes and robbing them while the people were on vacation. He had kept up with their schedules by people who filled out police forms to request police surveillance for their property while they were away. McDaniel had the file on your rape case. The file has been located, but the photos haven't been found. It seems you'll have to identify the attacker again or do an in-person lineup."

The thought depresses me. I think, So much for my stroke of luck. To Bonnie I say, sarcastically, "Wonderful! Story of my life."

Bonnie goes on to explain in detail the process of getting the attacker here for trial. "The guy had made it to Germany, where he was immediately placed in the stockade there. It seems the FBI had fingerprints of the rapist because of his military involvement. He is a paratrooper. They are having him extradited to the stockade at Fort Bragg, North Carolina. No official charges have been made and won't be until he gets back to the Tarrant County Jail, and then he should be arraigned on charges of Aggravated Sexual Assault with a Deadly Weapon, and Burglary of a Habitation. They are beginning the process of extradition now. Again, I caution you that he'll have to be re-identified some way in the near future."

Her words prove to be prophetic. On November 18, Officer David Oringderff of the Watauga Department of Public Safety contacts me regarding the identification I made of Lanny Gene Bevers, Jr., on July 20, when Captain McDaniel and Sergeant McCormick had visited my home. Officer Oringderff explains that the pictures I originally identified are missing. He doesn't tell me anything I didn't already know. I am glad Bonnie has prepared me.

On November 21, Officer Oringderff receives a set of five similar "mug shots" from the Tarrant County Sheriff's Office, one of which is Lanny Gene Bevers, Jr. Officer Oringderff randomly numbers and then initials the reverse side of each photo set, one through five; the suspect's photo bears the number three. Officer Oringderff proceeds to the Hurst Police Department and contacts Investigations. Officer Lily accompanies him to my office at the City of Hurst Service Center.

They ask me to look at the pictures to see if I can recognize anyone. I carefully look through the set of photos and pick the photo marked number three. I hand the photograph to Officer Oringderff, who asks, "Is this the man?"

"Yes," I simply reply. I think, Try not to lose this one.

"Are you sure?" asks Officer Oringderff.

I look straight into his eyes and steadily reply, "Absolutely, no doubt!"

This second identification of the same man is witnessed at 9:46 A.M., November 21, by Officers Lily and Oringderff. These photographs are sealed and placed with other evidence.

On Tuesday, November 22, the Tarrant County Grand Jury indicts Lanny Gene Bevers, Jr., for Aggravated Sexual Assault with a Deadly Weapon and Burglary of a Habitation. Bevers agrees to submit to a lie detector test administered by the Tarrant County Sheriff's Office. He fails it. I learn later that this piece of evidence is inadmissible in court, but it somehow makes me feel better, even relieved.

The last week of November, an assistant district attorney contacts me at my office. He suggests I call Jerry Buckner, who will be the lead prosecutor, and schedule an appointment to go over the facts of the case. He says that this is a good physical evidence case and will most likely go to trial.

On December 5, Mr. Buckner contacts Officer Oringderff to advise the officer he will be the prosecutor in the State vs. Lanny Gene Bevers, Jr. Mr. Buckner asks for pictures of the victim. He wants Karen Hunter's address. Further, he wants to know if anyone can place Bevers in the location on or about the day of the offense. Officer Oringderff offers that the gas station owner, Mr. Lindsey, had placed Bevers near the scene of the crime.

It is now near Christmas, which has always been a special holiday in my family. Our family shares our tree on Christmas

Eve every year and has dinner together on Christmas Day. For the first time in a long time, I put Bevers and the events created by him out of my mind.

After the holidays, the District Attorney's Office contacts me to schedule an appointment with Mr. Buckner. Subsequently, Aggie Wallace, the "hippie-looking" lady who had so unexpectedly shown up on my door step, befriends me. We find ourselves attending the same singles class at church. I ask her if she will testify at the trial.

Aggie acts very frightened and emphatically states, "Never! I could never do that!"

I ask why on earth she isn't interested in helping me get this guy off the streets. She astounds me by saying, "Look, La Vonne, I have two sons. I am a mother and have a mother's heart. Aside from being a little afraid, I know the Bevers family. I could never testify against someone I know, especially another mother's son."

I am overwhelmed.

Aggie drives me to the district attorney's office, where Mr. Buckner asks me if Aggie Wallace is willing to testify. He explains that her testimony about chasing Bevers out of her yard with an empty shotgun the night of the rape places him in the area and frame of mind. She still refuses. I find her attitude amazing!

My testimony is thoroughly discussed in preparation for the trial. I learn that our system of justice is a curious thing. Mr. Buckner advises me not to describe my house shoes as red. He is afraid it will give the wrong impression to certain jurors who may associate the color red with being risqué. Here I was in my own house, and I am made to feel guilty for having "risqué" house shoes. Oh, and he also strongly advises me to refer to my nightgown only as a nightgown and omit that it was pink. I surmise pink must be one of those sexy, risqué colors, too. I think to myself, Crazy system, huh? and shake my head.

We agree that Aggie's unwillingness to testify would make her a poor witness, even if she is subpoenaed. Mr. Buckner feels that my testimony, combined with the physical evidence, will be sufficient to make the case.

Chapter 5

The Trial

Bevers waives his plea bargain rights and requests a trial before a jury. The trial is slated to start Monday morning, the week of February 28, 1978. It will last one week.

Texas has a bifurcated jury system, whereby the defendant can select either a jury or judge to try him and, if he is found guilty, a jury or judge to sentence him. Bevers chooses the jury both to try him and to set punishment, in case of a guilty verdict. The trial is in Criminal District Court No. 4, with the Honorable Judge Gordon Gray presiding.

The courtroom is an intimate arena. The room is large, with a jury box on the left-hand side of the judge. Directly in front of the Judge's bench are two slightly smaller than conference-sized tables. This is where the prosecutors and defense attorneys sit. Almost like a wedding, the prosecutor and victim's supporters are seated to the right, while the defense team and the defendant's supporters are seated to the left.

The witness stand also is close to the Judge's immediate left, so the jury has a view of each witness. It is important that the jury be able to observe the witnesses and determine their truthfulness. The court reporter, who takes down every word that is said in the trial, sits facing the witness box, with his or her back to the jury. The door leading to the Judge's chambers is directly behind the jury box.

The jury room is behind and a little to one side of the Judge's bench. There is a swinging door on the left side of the rail that separates the court area, reserved for the Judge, court reporter, jury, defendant, his attorney, the prosecutor, and the witness box, from the spectator or gallery area. The defendant is placed at the far end of the defense table with his defense attorney to his right and the bailiff to his left. The door to the defendant's "holding cell" is to the Judge's right, on the left side of the courtroom.

The defense attorneys, Jack Garrett and Ben Trailor, are assisted by a young attorney, Danny Burns, who I already know. What a small world; I never expected a friendly acquaintance—in this case, Danny—to be defending the man who raped me.

The prosecutors are John Beatty, John Bankston, and Jerry Buckner. It is customary for the more seasoned, experienced prosecutor to serve as lead prosecutor. In this case, that is Mr. Buckner. He and his assistants have prepared me well for the trial. They explain that the defense attorneys probably will ask for "the rule" to be invoked, which means no witnesses are allowed in the courtroom to hear other testimony during the course of the trial. The purpose is to keep witnesses from hearing other testimony and tainting their own testimony by tailoring it to fit that of the other witnesses.

Ultimately, defense attorneys twist the purpose of "the rule" to help their client by keeping families of victims out of the court. "The rule" has been used many times for the sole purpose of keeping families of victims from hearing testimony and out of sight of the jurors. Another favorite defense tactic is for the defense attorney to swear in as a possible witness any "support" people for the victim, although the attorney has no intention whatsoever of calling those people to the witness stand. This keeps them out of the courtroom. "The rule" can be twisted into a flagrant abuse of the system to suit the purposes of the defense team.

Being the victim and a witness, I do not have the right to be present; however, it is interesting to note that the defendant—a potential witness—has the right to hear all the witnesses and conform his story to suit his situation. Because the burden of proof is on the State, the defendant is accorded the right of the presumption of innocence until proven guilty. Along with this right goes the right to face any witnesses or accusers against him.

Jury selection is about to begin in the rape trial of Army Private First Class Lanny Gene Bevers, Jr.

Mr. Buckner tells me to go straight to the witness room the first day of the trial. So I sit here with Bonnie, who drove me to the courthouse. It is a small, cold, bland little room, just off the side of the courtroom. There are a few hard chairs to sit on and one long table. It looks like a mini-conference room. There are no phones or magazines to help occupy the time. There is just a feeling of being shut off from the world.

I have copious notes that I have gone over with Mr. Buckner to refresh my memory. There are two assistants assigned to my case, but Mr. Buckner is in charge of the show. I am to learn that the attorneys have tunnel vision—the prosecutors want to win at all costs, and so do the defense attorneys. The prosecutors "divorce" themselves emotionally from the victim to keep their personal biases from causing them to make any errors.

I feel like I have been left totally out in the cold. My body is evidence, plain and simple. I have lost my sense of self-worth. It will take a long time to gain it back. As far as the court is concerned I am not even the injured party. "The People of Texas" are the injured party. I am merely a witness. I sure as hell feel like the injured party, and more than anything, I want Mr. Buckner to be my attorney, not the State's, but that just is not the way things work. I am warned not to leave my notes lying around for fear someone else may read them.

Mr. Buckner arrives prepared for battle, and looking like a "Greek god" to me. Premature gray hair dusts his temples. He reeks of charisma. He is commanding and self-assured.

I am pleased with the State's attorney and begin to relax a little bit. That feeling doesn't last long. Mr. Buckner comes out of the courtroom and opens the door to the witness room. He has a grave look on his face and I can tell he is not happy about what he has to tell me. "Brace yourself, La Vonne. Bevers is wearing his United States Army uniform."

What a shame to have a creep like this hide behind the American flag, looking clean and patriotic.

Mr. Buckner introduces me to the fingerprint expert who will be talking about the physical evidence. When Bevers picked up the glass from my kitchen door's window, he had been careless enough to leave a perfect fingerprint. Buckner says jurors love fingerprints. He had explained at his office that most jurors have a misconception about fingerprints, and that people, in general, think fingerprints are easily left behind by a defendant. They don't understand that a good, identifiable print is seldom found.

All the conditions have to be right to get a good fingerprint. The surface has to be right; the print can't be smeared or overlapped. However, if a prosecutor is fortunate enough, like in this case, where the defendant does leave behind a good fingerprint, he is almost guaranteed a guilty verdict.

The State's first witness is the fingerprint expert. He has a large, blown-up picture of the clearest fingerprint that the police had lifted from the glass. Fingerprints make the jurors' job easier because they don't have to agonize as to whether the testimony is credible. Fingerprints don't lie. This ought to do the trick, I figure.

Judge Gray enters the courtroom as the bailiff commands, "All rise; be seated." Judge Gray calls the court to order. All the witnesses are led in and stand behind the rail. They are told to raise their right hands and swear "to tell the truth and nothing but the truth, so help me God." The defense attorney stands and requests "the rule." The Judge, as expected, invokes "the rule." The Judge dismisses the witnesses with an admonishment not to discuss their testimony with anyone.

The bailiff leads the defendant into the courtroom and to the defense table, where his attorneys wait. As I turn to leave, I glance at the defendant. Sure enough, Bevers is wearing his uniform.

He looks smaller than I remember him, but then he doesn't have a thirteen-inch butcher knife today. He is thinner. I will later testify that I will never forget his piercing glare burn through to my soul. I am standing behind the rail approximately six feet away from Bevers. Although I have dreaded this moment, I feel surprisingly in control. I have a job to do, and an urgent need to get this man behind bars. It is important that Bevers does not perpetrate this kind of tragedy in another human's life.

All the witnesses return to the witness room. There is a rap on the door. I am so edgy, I jump. They are summoning the fingerprint expert.

The fingerprint expert testifies about the fifty-eight latent partial prints. He says only one print was clear enough to match the seven points required for identical identification with the defendant's prints. But one is all the State needs. The blown-up print provided by the FBI is shown to the jury. It is entered as the State's exhibit. The print is identified as belonging to Lanny Gene Bevers, Jr.

As I anxiously wait for my turn to testify, I can feel my heart pounding through my chest. My stomach churns with butterflies. My hands are cold. My mouth is dry. I am terrified, yet determined. As I wait, I pray that God will give me strength, the proper words to say, and help me recall all pertinent information. This time, when the bailiff knocks on the door, I know it is time for me to testify. Panic grips my gut, and a cold shudder goes down my spine.

Mr. Buckner has told me to expect to be on the stand approximately two hours. Before my ordeal on the stand is over, I will be called and recalled, examined and cross-examined, for a mind-boggling eight hours.

As I step up on the witness stand, Judge Gray reminds me that I am under oath. I take a deep breath and sit down. I glance at the jurors—praying they will believe every word I say.

What follows is taken directly from the court records, with the exception of my thoughts.

Mr. Buckner begins his questioning:

"Will you state your name, please?"

"Nancy Skalias."

"Where do you live, Mrs. Skalias?"

"1922 Presley Drive."

"Are you buying the place there?"

"Yes, I am."

"All right, Mrs. Skalias, I call your attention to the date of June 24, 1977, in the early morning hours. Do you recall an incident that occurred at that time?"

"Yes, sir, I most certainly do."

"Let me back up one more day, June 23. What time did you go to bed that night?"

"I went to bed at 9:00 A.M.—I'm sorry, 9:00 P.M. I was awakened—"

"About when?"

"About 2:00."

"What woke you up?"

"I heard the sound of glass breaking, and I jumped into my red slippers and ran to investigate, to see what was happening. And, when I reached my hall, I flipped on my light, and I could hear my door swinging open."

"What clothing were you wearing at that time?"

"I had on a regular, shorty nightgown, and I had on underwear, bra and panties."

"When you flipped on the light and you heard your door open, what happened next, or what did you see next?"

"I saw a young man standing there with a knife, and he had grabbed me and put the knife up in the air with a blade pointing downward."

Buckner continues: "And I call your attention to the defendant on trial here today, Lanny Gene Bevers, Jr., seated at defense table in the Army uniform. Is that the man you saw that night?"

"Yes."

"Do you have any doubt whatsoever?"

"None."

"What did he say or do next?"

"He said for me not to scream."

"Using his exact words, if you would, please."

"Well, some of it was obscenity. Would I have to say it?"

"Yes, ma'am. As I instructed you previously, the jury has to know exactly what went on and what his words were so that they'll be in the same position you were in that night and understand it. What did he say?"

"He told me not to scream; that he would hurt my daughter and myself and he said that 'I have a hard dick and I'm going to fuck you.'"

A break is called and then the testimony resumes.

Buckner begins: "Did you fight him as hard as you could until you realized that death was imminent?"

"I thought that he would kill or mutilate or do something—some terrible thing to myself or my little girl. I just couldn't allow that to happen. I knew that God wouldn't."

"Mrs. Skalias, did the defendant, Lanny Gene Bevers, Jr., ever make the statement to you, 'All women are alike'?"

"Yes, he did. In trying to keep him from being violent, I kept him talking as much as I could during the rape."

"Had you ever seen this man before in your life before that night when this took place?"

"No."

"Do you run around in bars and honky-tonks?"

"No."

After hours on the witness stand, Mr. Buckner has one last question for me.

"Do you have any doubt in your mind whatsoever that this defendant sitting over there at the counsel table in the paratrooper's uniform, Lanny Gene Bevers, Jr., is the one that did the things that you say happened to you between 2:00 and 3:00 A.M. on June 24, 1977?"

"There is no doubt in my mind!"

Mr. Buckner: "I pass the witness, your Honor."

Next the defense attorney, Mr. Garrett, begins cross-examining me.

"Would you describe your house as sort of a Spanish theme, is that correct? Would that be correct?"

"Spanish to contemporary."

"On the windows outside your house—I don't know anything about the size or the back or anything like that. They have grates on them, or bars, is that correct?"

"Yes, I have had bars put on since the break-in."

"That was since then?"

"Right. On the front of the house for decoration. They had put some little bars that were just, you know, to give it the Spanish quality—the look to the house, but since that has been done, I spent about $407 to the penny to get bars put on by an ironworks place, and then I bought a Genie."

Mr. Garrett's questions continue nonstop:

"I would like to know in what area was the first time that you saw this person that grabbed you?"

"Okay. He was coming through the family room, the living room, the den area."

"At that time, you also said something to the effect, 'Do you believe in God' to him?"

"I had asked him if he believed in God, and he told me, 'Lady, I don't believe in God. God ain't never done nothing for me.'"

"Now, then, the butcher knife he has in his hand all of this time, is that correct?"

"He had put the butcher knife in his boot when we went into the back bathroom. He did not put the knife outside the door until after my clothing was taken off."

"At the time that I drove by your house—and I understand why—these garage doors were heavily padlocked?"

"I keep it padlocked. I have always kept a padlock on the left garage door, even the night of the break-in; however, I had lost the padlock for the door on the right, and that is when I had used a board that went across both doors. Now, since this has occurred, I have little metal bars. They are iron bars that go across the windows on the garage doors now."

"Are you saying that the padlock to this right-hand door had been lost for some time?"

"Yes. And I had not replaced it. I never—I'm just like anybody else. I just didn't think anything like this would happen to me. It's always somebody else you read about and hear about."

Mr. Garrett begins getting more grueling with his questions:

"In your best estimation, pinpoint down, the best that you can do, the length of the attack. Would you say three minutes?"

"I would say longer than that."

"Five minutes?"

"I would say in length of—say, five to ten minutes. That is the best I can give. Maybe not even ten minutes. I'm not positive. I can't really say the length of time. It's something like that."

"Ten minutes is a long fight."

"Even a minute, when you're going through any kind of problem, feels like an eternity."

"And then we had the bandaging of the finger. The hunt—he hunting and you hunting for a bandage. He bandaged your finger. How much additional time there?"

"Well, there was—looking through the medicine cabinet that he did, and then I knew the bandages were in my bureau drawer, and I walked back to the linen closet. I had to get a towel and so forth to wash the blood off. We were walking around. It could have been—"

"Five minutes? Four minutes?"

Mr. Buckner: "I'm going to object to him arguing with the witness about the length of time. She's already stated, and she's already testified that she saw 3:00 A.M. on her digital clock when she called her friends."

The Court: "Sustained."

Mr. Buckner: "Thank you, sir."

Mr. Garrett: "Just so that I won't run into—am I now forbidden to ask her anymore about the sequence of time?"

My head swirls with the confusion going on around me.

The Court: "She said she didn't know. I've sustained the objection."

Mr. Garrett: "I'm forbidden from—"

The Court: "You understand the ruling, don't you?"

Mr. Garrett: "That is what I was trying to do, clarify it."

The Court: "She said she didn't know. She answered the question, so you can't ask it again."

Mr. Garrett: "Is that confined to the time looking for the bandage or the entire time that —"

The Court: "Go ahead and ask her and I'll take it up when I get to it. You ask whatever you want to."

By the time the Court and Mr. Garrett finish their round-for-round, I am dizzy.

Mr. Garrett: "Now, then, Mrs. Skalias, after the bandage—passing from that, how long would you say that you were in the back bathroom?"

"Again, time element is difficult. I would say that we were probably—this is just an estimate. I can't really say it's a fact. We may have been in there fifteen, twenty minutes. Most of it was talking conversation trying to keep him from becoming violent. There were acts of penetration that took place and there were obscene things that was said."

Mr. Buckner then redirects: "Mrs. Skalias, I just have a few more questions and that'll be all we have for you. The defense pointed out to you on page two—if you will turn to that page of your statement where the defense attorney pointed out specifically that he [Bevers] kept on apologizing and that he bandaged your finger, and I would like to call your attention to his next statement immediately following that, which the defense attorney did not choose to bring out. What did he say after it was bandaged?"

"He said, 'Let's get on with it.' He told me he was horny and he was facing a twenty-year prison sentence. And he missed being with women and he wanted it to be good because he knew that he would be away for awhile."

After a few more questions, Mr. Buckner passes the witness to Mr. Garrett for further recross-examination. I am beginning to feel a little like a football, with all the passing back and forth.

Mr. Garrett: "When is the last time that you talked to your lawyer, Mr. Buckner?"

"Well, we have gone over my statement."

"Have you talked with him within the last forty-five minutes or hour-and-a-half?"

Mr. Buckner: "Your Honor, I stipulate that I talked to her during the recess. Of course I did."

Mr. Garrett: "At that time, he brought out to you and suggested to you about this moustache, didn't he? You didn't testify about the moustache on direct examination testimony. He mentioned that moustache to you, didn't he?"

A little confused with the game-playing going on around me, I answer: "He asked me if there was anything else about his upper lip. If there was hair."

"About his upper lip?"

"Yes, but I do know—"

"You didn't say anything about that on direct examination, but you remembered it when Mr. Buckner suggested it to you about his upper lip?"

"I had given my description to the Watauga Police, that the man had a growth of hair, more like fuzz, on the upper lip, and it should have been in the record."

"I understand as to what happened now. You say, Mrs. Skalias, that you kept your garage door opened—"

Mr. Buckner: "Your Honor, may Counsel's side-bar remark please be stricken from the record?"

The Court: "I'll instruct the jury not to consider it."

The battering continues and goes into a full-blown storm when the issue of the two photo spreads erupts. The jury is escorted out of the courtroom, where questioning continues out of their presence:

Mr. Garrett: "And you say in no way whatsoever did Captain McDaniel influence your decision?"

"Captain McDaniel did nothing to influence my decision, one way or the other. He just stood there and spread the pictures out on the table and said, 'Can you identify any of these men?' period."

"He didn't do it in a subtle manner?"

"No. He stood back, and Officer McCormick stood there, and I did the work. I had to look at them and go over it. It was terribly painful, but I went through them. I did everything I knew to do, because I knew what I wanted was the person that did this off the street."

Mr. Garrett: "Pass the witness."

Mr. Buckner flies to his feet, and says, "Your Honor, we submit that the witness should be able to testify before the jury as to her previous identification of the defendant in the two photographic lineups."

Mr. Garrett indignantly stands and says, "Your Honor, I submit that it's impossible. This lady doesn't know anything at all other than she looked at some pictures out here. We don't have Captain McDaniel here to testify; they haven't tried to introduce the first photo spread, so that we can have an opportunity ourselves or the defendant can have an opportunity to see whether or not these are like or similar people that was presented to her. We just have her testimony here. That would inflame the minds of these jurors, if the photos were introduced. They have one photo session; they don't have Captain McDaniel or his photo spread. I say that the first photo session influenced the second. Unless they can establish the first one was good, I don't think the second photo session is any good either. We object to the introduction!"

The Court: "I'll overrule the objection. It's admissible."

Mr. Buckner: "Thank you, your Honor. May we have the jury brought back in?"

The Court: "Okay, bailiff, bring the jury back in."

After the jury is seated, a further redirect examination takes place from Mr. Buckner:

"Prior to Friday, June the 24th, I think that you said you had never seen Lanny Bevers before, is that correct?"

"Never before that . . . before he broke in my house."

"And you haven't seen him in person since that night, is that correct?"

"Correct. Except in the pictures."

"Except in the pictures."

Mr. Buckner: "Pass the witness."

Mr. Garrett: "No further questions, your Honor."

JUDGE GRAY TURNS TO ME and politely tells me I may step down. What a relief! I am shaking as a bailiff ushers me out of the courtroom and back to the cold, steel witness room, now a peaceful respite from the battling ground of the courtroom. I will stay here until the jury reaches a verdict.

After heated objections punctuate closing arguments from both sides, Mr. Garrett and Mr. Buckner rest their cases and put it in the hands of the jurors. After two-and-a-half hours of deliberation the jury has not reached a verdict, so Judge Gray sends them home with the admonishment not to read about the incident or watch any news on the television regarding this trial. The jury returns to deliberate Thursday at 9:00 A.M.

DURING THE TIME I AM IN THE WITNESS ROOM, I am not allowed to monitor what is happening in the courtroom.

Later, though, I read newspaper accounts that say Bevers's mother took the stand to bolster her son's claims that he was innocent in the rape. Mrs. Carol Bevers Baker testifies that she was raped by a young man, who bore a close physical resemblance to her son, just four months after my rape.[1]

Mr. Buckner refutes her testimony by bringing forth the fingerprint evidence found inside my home on the piece of glass the attacker had picked up.

Bevers's attorney argues in final arguments that the victim was simply mistaken in her identity of Bevers as her assailant. He contends that Bevers was with two women who were each called to the stand and each, in turn, said Mr. Bevers was with them at the time in question of the assault. He further adds that Mr. Bevers had sufficiently explained how his fingerprints had gotten on the kitchen door's window.

I hear that Bevers had taken the stand and made up some preposterous story about my having seen him sunbathing in his front yard, and subsequently fell madly in love with him. He says this was the story of a woman scorned because he did not return her affections. Of course, he has nothing but an active imagination to back up this claim. Bevers claims his mom's black poodle had run into my garage, and that he believed I had taken the pooch in. He further claims he had propped himself up to reach behind some old discarded boxes to peer into the house to see if the dog was there. In his version, his fingerprints got on the kitchen door window by pressing his palms against the glass to look inside for the lost dog.

[1] *Fort Worth Star-Telegram*, March 1-3, 1978.

THE JURY IS BACK. They pronounce Lanny Gene Bevers, Jr., guilty of Aggravated Sexual Assault with a Deadly Weapon. As the verdict is read, he glances back at me. I will never forget his hate-filled glare. I will be allowed back in to hear the jury sentence him.

On March 4, 1978, the jury, unimpressed by Bevers's testimony, sentences him to a twenty-year maximum sentence in prison for Aggravated Sexual Assault with a Deadly Weapon. Bevers goes to prison denying his guilt.

Chapter 6

Back to Normal

I am appalled that the sentence is so light. Twenty years just does not seem to be harsh enough for all Bevers has taken from me. I remember they once put to death such criminals in Texas; now I wonder why they changed the law.

Everyone keeps telling me how fortunate I am to come out of such a horrible crime with just a few scratches. I know they can never understand the way I feel now or felt then, but with the attacker locked away, I do feel safer.

Michelle and I try to pick up the pieces of our shattered lives. During the coming years I attempt to re-create a balance of normalcy. Our activities center around work, school, picnics, holidays; all the normal things people should be able to do.

There is a new sense of security with Bevers locked away. I am pretty sure that Michelle will be grown and married before he will have an opportunity to enter our lives again.

Over the next few years, I work at various secretarial jobs. From time to time I get in discussions about whether I should pack up my things, take Michelle, and leave this place I call home. I can deal with the memories; it is the fear that he will return that haunts me.

The police, Rape Crisis, and friends all tell me it would be foolish to uproot my daughter and myself. They assure me that rapists often threaten to get back at their victims, but seldom carry out the threats.

With a modicum of peace of mind, I decide to suppress my fear of Bevers's threats and stay. Michelle will soon be old enough to go to junior high school, and Watauga Junior High School is only a couple of blocks away. Michelle also has many friends and doesn't want to leave the only home she has ever known.

We go about our lives fairly carefree of any real threat of danger from Bevers. After all, the police tell me that the Texas Parole Board will notify me before they release someone as dangerous as Bevers. With that in mind, I try to live a normal life for Michelle's sake and my own.

Part II

Reliving a
Nightmare

Chapter 7

Night of Revenge

"**I**'ll get you and kill you when I get out, if you tell on me." The last words Bevers had spoken to me after he raped me in 1977 still haunt me. I just can't get those words off my mind.

It is now early September 1984. My anxiety about Bevers returning has been abated by Rape Crisis, the police department, and friends. They assured me shortly after the rape trial that fewer than 1 percent of rapists ever retaliate. However, the fear of him returning lingers, quietly plaguing me. I sleep uneasy, remembering Bevers's threat and the look in his eyes when he heard the guilty verdict more than six years ago.

In my naiveté about the judicial system, I calculate Bevers has fourteen more years to serve on his twenty-year sentence. I try to feel secure and go on with my life. He has stolen enough time from me.

I work as a secretary for a different local school district, and with school back in session, I am extremely busy. Friday, September 7, 1984, is a chaotic day. As I walk in the door, Michelle's familiar giggle permeates the air. Now almost twelve years old, she is again talking on the phone. I am tired and looking forward to a relaxing, quiet weekend. I go to my room and remove my outer clothes, throwing a nightgown over my undergarments like a house dress. I think, I'll change before bed.

After dinner, Michelle does her homework and retires for the night. No longer a child, she fiercely protects her privacy by keeping her door closed. As is my usual habit, I check all the doors before going to bed. After the rape in 1977, I added iron bars to every door and window, and enclosed the sliding patio door with bars. All of this makes me feel more secure.

Ominously, the automatic garage door opener—repaired after the attack in 1977—broke again just a couple of days ago. I nag my dad to fix it until he calls the service department. They tell him it will be a few days before they can make it out. Nevertheless, ensconced in my fortress, I feel safe.

Ready to relax, I reach in the refrigerator, pull out a Dr. Pepper, and head for my bedroom. I set the drink on the nightstand beside the bed. Shifting through the clothes in the closet, I retrieve a dark-colored blouse and a pair of jeans, and place them at the foot of the bed. With tomorrow off, I plan to relax and go fishing with a friend. The blouse and jeans will be perfect to wear.

I climb into bed still wearing my nightgown, bra, panties, and pantyhose. Settling under the sheets, I reach for the phone and make a few calls. After talking to my mom, I call my close friends, R. C. and Vinita Kemp, who know both Larry, my fiancé, and me. As they talk, the Kemps, being on different extensions, take turns consoling me long into the night. An argument I had with Larry dominates our conversation.

After hanging up the phone, I get up and close the bedroom door—another habit acquired after the rape—and turn out the ceiling light. I want as many barriers as possible between myself and an intruder. I consider taking off my undergarments, but it seems too much of a bother. I glance at the clock on the nightstand. It is a few minutes past midnight.

The conversation about my fiancé agitated me. I feel restless and decide to read. An hour or so later, I lay the book on the nightstand and turn out the lamp. Sporadic, troubling dreams periodically jerk me out of my sleep. The bad dreams have increased with the rumors that Bevers has been or soon will be paroled. Assurances by law enforcement personnel that it is too soon for him to be released do not suppress my fears.

Troublesome dreams snatch me from sleep. By my clock it is 2:58 A.M. Wanting to feel rested for the fishing trip, I shrug off the dream and attempt to slip back to sleep.

I am lying on my left side of the far right-hand side of the king-size bed when the loud crash of my closed and locked bedroom door being kicked in awakens me. My eyes quickly adjust to the darkness, enabling me to discern a silhouetted figure springing through the air and onto my bed. The sight petrifies me. My heart is pounding so hard I fear I am having a heart attack. Terror spreads through me like a brush fire.

A man with a stocking covering his head pounces on the left side of the bed. He is in a wild frenzy and begins slashing at me with a knife. As he grabs me, a terrifying scream erupts from my mouth and pierces the silence. Turning me, he whispers in a raspy voice, "Roll over on your stomach, now!" Fear grips my very soul!

His fingers grasp my hair and yank my head back while he tucks away the knife in his back pocket. The next thing I am aware of is the barrel of a gun pressing hard against my temple. I can feel the pressure of the barrel baring down against my head. I hear the sound of the gun's hammer as it is cocked. The intruder proclaims, "This is a .44 magnum, and I'm going to blow your fucking brains out!" Paralyzed by fear, I can see the chambers of the gun and the intruder's gloves as his finger presses against the trigger. The panic within me swells. I believe every word he says.

Things are happening fast! He pushes me back against the headboard, securing me with one hand while he places the gun on the nightstand. It terrifies me, but I do not know what to do. I think to try and grab the gun, but recall the knife and decide against it.

Desperately, I try to grasp the reality of what is happening. Rapists don't come back. It can't be Bevers; he is still in prison. This is just a dream. It cannot be happening again...not to me...not to me!

I fight back with all my strength, but he ends my struggle quickly by retrieving the gun and striking my right temple twice with considerable force using its butt. God, what pain! Blood gushes from the wound and temporarily blinds me. Instinctively, I curl up in a fetal position, trying to protect myself from further injury.

Having subdued me, he puts the gun back on the night-stand and takes the knife out of his back pocket, slashing at the sheets using a zigzag pattern. Defensively, I raise my hand in front of my face to deflect the blade. I feel a painful cut on the thumb of my left hand as the sharp edge of the knife grazes it. I bury my head into the pillow to keep him from slashing my face.

He pries me free and effortlessly flips me over on my side. I am paralyzed, horrified, thinking about his possible next move.

He twists my arm behind my back, holding my right hand in a painful vise-like grip. I scream from the excruciating pain as he digs into my wrist, eventually bellowing like a wounded animal. The pain is agony, and I tremble as he gets off the bed and reaches for the gun.

I know this man is here to kill me! I have to get away from him. Seeing my chance to escape, I fling my legs off the side of the bed. My feet hit the floor just as a gunshot explodes and reverberates through the room. My God, I'm shot! My hands fly to my chest to feel for the wound, but I feel no blood. The bullet has narrowly missed its target, detouring through the center of the mattress and out of the box springs.

I realize God has spared me. I have not been hit. Thinking only of escape, I run for my life through the hall toward the kitchen door. In my haste to flee, I bump my shin on the organ bench. I wince, but continue my flight. The kitchen is pitch black. My heart hammers against my rib cage as I reach out with my right hand and frantically turn the knob on the kitchen door leading to freedom. Unable to turn it, I try again and again. Something is wrong! My hand just will not grip the knob without slipping off. What the hell, I wonder as I realize time is running out. I am becoming hysterical. I feel something warm and sticky running down my right arm. Stubbornly, I work again on opening the door. Then panic overwhelms me.

Confused by my inability to turn the knob and open the door, I reach over with my left hand and flip on the light. I look down at my right hand. Horror grips me. My face turns ashen. My mouth twists in an expression of disbelief as I suppress the urge to vomit. I lift the hand to my face. Warm blood floods down my wrist and forearm. My thumb is gone! It has been completely severed to the base of the wrist. I gag at the sight of the mutilation.

Fighting my mounting fear, I reach for the knob with my left hand, fling the door open and start into the garage. But he is behind me now. I feel his arm around my waist. I let out a yelp. He is pulling me through the doorway back into the house.

In sheer desperation, I throw my arms and legs out in a spread-eagle formation. I try futilely to wedge myself in the doorway and block him from pulling my body back through. With one vigorous tug he dislodges me. We both land in a heap in the middle of the kitchen floor.

He kicks me off of him and clambers to his knees. He notices my hand and sneers, "Oh, look, you've cut your thumb off! Guess you better clean up that blood."

Laughing, he bends down and pins my arms on the floor as he begins to interrogate me. "Who are you?"

I answer, "I'm La Vonne."

He pursues, "What's your first name?"

I don't know why, but I lie, telling him it is Sally.

He angrily snaps back, "You're not Sally, you're Nancy. Aren't you, Nancy?"

I nod. A wave of terror sweeps over me as I hear him call me by my first name. At this moment, I know the attacker is Lanny Bevers. He has kept his promise. This is my notice from the parole board that Bevers is a free man. I think, This is it…I'm dead!

He continues, "You're thirty-nine years old now. Where's Michelle?" Petrified at the mention of my daughter's name, I lie again, telling him she isn't here. He looks at me intensely, clenches his teeth, and scowls. Then, once again, he asks, "Where is she?"

I insist she is spending the night with friends. I pray to God Michelle does not come out of her room.

Hoping to divert his attention from Michelle, I begin to bargain with him—if he'll leave, I will not call the police. He laughs at me. Desperate, I switch tactics. "You'd better leave," I warn. "My husband is due home in ten minutes."

Unfazed, he replies, "Good. He's a dead man, too!"

Dear God, nothing I am saying is working. I'm going to die! I'm going to die! Standing up, he reaches down and grabs a handful of my hair and uses it to hoist me painfully to my feet. Pushing me in the back with his hands, he prods me every few feet in the direction he wants. "Get into the bathroom, bitch!" he barks.

When he shoves too hard, I lose my balance and fall. Twisting his fingers around my hair, using it like a handle, he maneuvers me into the direction of the bathroom. Dragging me down the hall, he asks, "How long's it been since you been fucked good?"

Why me? Why again? Haven't I suffered enough? Save me, Lord, save me! He stops as we reach the bathroom by the hall, releasing my hair. The bathroom light is on, and he orders me not to look at him as I manage to get to my feet. Walking past the mirror, I notice the glint of a gold chain around his neck, then quickly avert my eyes, moving—as he instructs—toward the tub.

He orders me to turn on the water. As he shouts commands at me to hurry, I start turning on both faucets. When the water is halfway to the top of the tub, I turn the faucets off.

He directs me to sit in the tub. I am trembling from fear, but climb in obediently. As he picks up my injured hand I see that the blood is beginning to coagulate around the wound, but it is still bleeding. He roughly shoves the hand under the water, causing it to bleed profusely. The blood turns the clear water a deep, crimson red.

He notices for the first time that I am wearing pantyhose. Angry, he takes out the knife and begins cutting them off. Just seeing the knife again terrifies me. As he rips the nylons, I pull them from his clutch and quickly roll the pieces up in my hands. He then notices my underwear. Enraged, he screams, "You still have your panties on!"

Clutching me around the throat, he shoves me against the back of the tub. My heart starts racing as he slides the knife under the right side of my panties, slitting them apart with its sharp edge. Then he slits the other side and yanks the panties off with his knife. Still on the knife blade, he flings them to the floor.

I watch in horror as he snatches the remaining pantyhose from my hands. My mind starts recording his actions in slow motion. I watch him methodically wrap the nylons around his hands and form a ligature. He's going to strangle me! I reach up just in time to place my fingers between my neck and the pantyhose as he twists them tightly around my throat. Desperately, I fight to keep my oxygen supply from being cut off.

As the battle rages, I think, I'm not going to die this way. He pulls the stockings tighter. Struggling, I slap at him with my free hand, which becomes entangled in the gold chain on his neck. As I fight for my life, the chain breaks and falls to the bottom of the water.

When the chain snaps, it is like he snaps; the battle ceases as quickly as it began. Exhausted, I slump down in the water. Holding my throat with both hands, I gasp urgently for air. The intense struggle has moved my bra up around the top of my breasts. As he backs away, a smile that says, "Death won't come that easy," creeps across his face.

I watch as he goes to the linen closet, gets a towel, then walks back to the tub. He dips it in the bloody water and wrings it out. With the towel still dripping, he starts wiping down my bedroom door facing, then bends down and rubs the towel across the carpet. Fear overwhelms me. I can't imagine what all he has in store for me.

He stands and looks back at me, smirking, then shrewdly walks to Michelle's door. He begins slowly wiping the door with the blood-soaked towel. Understanding the mental impact his actions have on me, he reaches for the doorknob and starts slightly opening then shutting the door. He keeps repeating this action as if he is trying to scare me to death. The hysteria surges through my body. I repeatedly pray, "Please, God, let him leave Michelle alone! Take me, but not Michelle…not my baby!"

He abandons this form of torture for the moment and returns to the linen closet, where he takes out more towels. He sits down on the floor outside of Michelle's room. I am terrified and bewildered. I watch as he takes out a cigarette lighter. One by one he holds up the towels and proceeds to burn holes in them, quickly snuffing out each fire before the flames engulf the towel.

As soon as he completes this task, he returns to scouring the walls with the towel. The closer he gets to Michelle's door, the more upset I become. I know I have to distract him; get his mind off Michelle.

Scared to death, I slip part way out of the tub, but scramble back in as he turns to check on me. I do this several times before I manage the courage and control to get all the way out of the tub. I crouch down, waiting for a chance to run.

He fixates on a religious plaque hanging on the wall that is opposite and a little ways down from the bathroom. He is polishing it in a circular motion, over and over, with the bloody towel. I seize the opportunity, quietly slip by him, then break out in a run toward the front door, stopping only long enough to grab the key ring next to my purse on the couch. I try to stop shaking as I fumble with the keys, searching for the one that unlocks the iron bars. My heart leaps when I find it. I hold my breath, hoping he will not hear as I quietly open the front door.

He does hear and yells, "Lady, what are you doing? Where are you going?" I am despondent and my heart pounds rapidly as I try to get out before he can get to me. I get the key in the lock of the iron gate and turn it, expecting to be free. It doesn't work. Desperate, I shake the bars. I am confused as to why they will not open, then I realize I have turned the key the wrong way. I am trying to operate with my left hand and it isn't working too well. Before I can turn the key in the opposite direction, I hear him coming up behind me, issuing the directive, "Nancy, get away from that door!" My hopes plummet; I had been seconds away from freedom.

I hide the keys behind my back, take a deep breath, and lie, "It's all right. I just need some fresh air. Please let me get some air."

Pushing me aside, he slams the front door shut and scolds me, "Get away from this door!" He turns and starts toward the living room. With his back to me, I carefully slip the keys under a throw pillow on the couch. A can of mace is attached to the key ring, but remembering his weapons, I quickly reject the notion of using it.

As he glances back at me his personality seems to change. He apologizes in a soft voice, "Lady, if you wouldn't have fought me, I wouldn't have hurt you so bad." Wandering away, he starts wiping the organ keys and the top of the piano with the bloody towel, then moves on to the living room walls.

Engrossed in his activities, he does not notice as I run to the bedroom and awkwardly pick up the phone to call for help. Holding the phone to my ear, I listen, disbelieving the silence. My finger rapidly clicks the button on the phone up and down. There is no dial tone.

His footsteps warn me of his approach and I quickly replace the receiver and look around for an escape route. I cannot find one. He calls out and demands to know what I am doing. I feel like a cornered animal and mumble that I am looking for bandages and something for pain. I open the dresser to bolster my lie. He mistakes my motives and starts shouting, "Where's your gun? Where's the gun at?"

He begins pulling dresser drawers open, frantically searching for a weapon. Finding nothing in the dresser drawers, he continues his search and tosses a pillow off the bed.

As he is conducting his search, I look around to try and figure out my next move. I spot his cigarette lighter. It is lying on the carpet among the collection of shoes I have gathered for Goodwill and deposited at the base of the chest of drawers. Cautiously, I work my way around the bed, then break out in a run. He captures me almost immediately. We grapple at the foot of the bed before I manage to wrench myself free.

I bolt toward the kitchen, determined to escape. Hearing him come up behind me, I vow, "He's not stopping me this time." As I reach the kitchen door leading out to the garage, I lock my feet solidly against the door facings. I know he is close behind me. His strength is much greater than mine. Wrapping his arms around my waist, he unlocks my right foot by kicking it hard into the doorjam, breaking my tibia upon impact and crushing my ankle bone. He slams the door with an immense force into my right leg. Wanting to punish my defiance, he opens the door and smashes it, as hard as he can, once more against my leg.

There is a sickening crack as my bones give way under the pressure of the door. It hurts so bad I am unable to cry out.

Instead, I feel myself go faint. As one of the broken bones protrudes through my leg, a piercing white flash of light accompanies the pain. He slams the door again, breaking my ankle. He shoves the door with all his weight against the outer portion of my right leg, shattering the fibula. I see the protruding bone and feel myself falling to the floor. I pass out from the excruciating pain.

Lying on the kitchen floor, I drift in and out of consciousness. Each time I awake, I hear a loud tapping noise on the kitchen table, before fading once more into oblivion. When I am momentarily awake, I turn my head and observe him sitting at the kitchen table. Every time I open my eyes, I pray the monster will be gone—but he never disappears.

I come around slowly, as the tapping stops. I follow the voice as he walks toward me. Brazenly he declares, "You know, I could cut you into little bitty pieces, put you in a garbage bag, and dump your body all over Denton County. They'd never find you. Serial killers like old Henry Lee Lucas knew how to handle women!"

Without warning, I feel the sickening sensation as his two fingers forcibly enter my vagina. He starts bragging, "You're ready for me to fuck you, aren't you, bitch?" I get sick as he begins spreading my legs further apart. He tries cramming his limp penis in me, gloating, "You want it, baby, don't you?" After several attempts, he fails to penetrate me. Angry, he shouts, "I bet you want it in the ass!" I cannot believe this nightmare is happening again. Slipping out of me, he forcefully pushes both my legs back toward my head. Unbearable pain shoots through my broken limb. Flinching from the tremendous pain, I try to brace myself. God! My hand aches as it touches the floor. No longer recognizable, the bloody, swollen hand appears to have been torn apart by a carnivorous animal.

Tears well in my eyes, as I weep for myself. "Why me, my God? Why me? Let death come. Bring it swiftly, dear God," I pray as tears begin to fall down my cheeks; tears for my family, and even my attacker, who has become such an intricate part of my life. What happened to make him so full of hate, so devoid of feelings? How could someone do this to another human being? How could…my thoughts are interrupted as he lifts my bottom slightly off the floor.

The rage in him turns his penis into the weapon he has yearned for. As he jams himself into my rectum, I feel myself being ripped apart. A low groan crawls from the bottom of my lungs, erupting from my mouth into a shrill scream as Bevers sodomizes me. He is totally out of control.

Listening to my screams, Michelle huddles in the bed in her room and cups her hands over her ears to drown out the horror of it all. The security bars block her exit through the window. Her only escape route is through the hall. Not knowing what this man is doing to her mother to evoke such agonizing screams, uncertain if she will be next, tears stream down her cheeks as she sobs and rocks back and forth.

Bevers soon loses his erection and pulls out of me. He callously jerks my legs back down and straddles my chest, pinning my arms underneath his legs. Holding his penis, he shouts, "All right, you bitch, suck it!" As he forces his penis into my mouth, I start to gag. He says, "You better make it good, bitch." I suppress the urge to bite down as hard as I can. It has been a long time since I have been in a violent confrontation. I know if I don't bite hard enough, simply wounding him, he'll kill me right here. By now, though, death for me seems almost a relief.

Intruding on my dilemma, he shouts again, "Suck it, bitch!" Not wanting to please him, but not quite ready to die, I make a feeble attempt to quell his anger by moving my head back and forth as he continues to shout at me. As the rage within him grows, I know he hates me...hates all women...just like he told me when he raped me before.

My neck begins to hurt so I rest my head on the floor. Exhausted and sobbing, I wonder what will happen when he is done. Pain emanates from my body as I hold my eyes tightly closed. Bevers still has not climaxed when he withdraws from my mouth.

Bending down over my prone body, he carefully lifts the stocking mask, revealing only his lips and a slight wisp of a moustache—like the one he had in 1977. When he attempts to kiss me, I clamp my lips shut and turn my head to avoid his mouth. I think there are no further indignities he can force on me; however, I soon learn otherwise as he begins to work his way down my body, licking it. My stomach heaves each time his tongue laps at my skin. Spreading my legs wider apart, he begins to perform oral sex on me. Staring up at the ceiling, tears trickling down my face, I contemplate whether a bullet would have been preferable.

When he is through, he raises back up and gives me a hard kiss, sticking his tongue deep inside my mouth. God, I want to vomit! Getting off of me, he stands up triumphantly and zips his pants. Leering at this terrified woman on the floor, he can't resist one last jab as he arrogantly remarks, "You want some more, bitch, cause I can give you some more." Sobbing, I slowly shake my head.

My body is wracked with pain as I lie on the floor, broken and mutilated. My brain quickly attempts to assess the damage. My leg is shattered in two places, and the bone is protruding through the skin at one break; my head is busted from the butt of a gun; my thumb is severed; and I have been raped in every conceivable manner.

There is nothing left he can do to me. I know he is ready to kill me now, and I whisper, "Let me come to you, dear Jesus. I'm ready." But Bevers is not ready. He has just completed the defiling of my body. He is now ready to commence with the mind games.

Seizing me by the hair, he jerks me halfway up, shrieking, "Walk, bitch, walk! Come on, Nancy, walk!" I feebly pull myself up the rest of the way by bracing myself with the uninjured side of my body. Holding on to his shoulders and shirt, I slowly take a step while clinging to the enemy for support.

The shattered bone in my leg is protruding completely through the skin, making walking almost impossible. I drag the useless limb, trying to keep the bone from jutting out any further, and hop on the other leg. I have only gone a short distance when, without warning, Bevers jumps completely away from my body, causing me to lose what little balance I have and fall.

Laughing, he asks, "What's the matter, bitch, can't you walk?" He acts disgusted with me as he bends down and hauls me back up on my feet, lets me struggle to walk a little further, and once again lets go of me, causing me to tumble to the floor. He laughs out loud and again asks, "Having trouble walking, bitch?"

This diversion begins to bore him. He grasps me by the hair on my head and begins dragging me through the living room, smashing my broken body into the furniture like a rag doll. I cry out each time my broken leg or injured hand makes contact with anything.

Once we make it into the hall, he reaches under my arms and pulls me the rest of the way into the bathroom, propping me up against the sink and then letting me go. With no one to support me, I slip on the mixture of blood and water that covers the floor, and land hard on my tailbone. Finding this humorous, Bevers snickers and smugly says, "Oops, you're just gonna have to be more careful," then adds, "Get up, bitch!"

Aching all over, but too frightened not to comply, I somehow manage to pull myself up by clutching his pant leg and then his shirt. After I slowly and painstakingly make it to my feet, he twists my arm—sparing no pain—behind my back and situates me in front of the mirror—as he had done before. This time, instead of a butcher knife, he shoves the barrel of the .44 magnum roughly under my chin. The barrel of the gun is pressed so hard against my skin it leaves a quarter-size bruise. He gives his standard order not to look at him. His eyes are filled with hatred as he proclaims, "I ought to kill you, Nancy." I remember those words from before.

Cautiously, I observe him out of the corner of my eye. I see his head shaking. During this brief respite from battering me, I take the opportunity to observe more about him. I have to keep thinking…keep my mind from breaking as he has broken my body. The best way to do this is for me to observe him as closely as possible and take mental notes.

The stocking covering his head consists of several pantyhose tied together with the knot flopping to the right side of his neck; the remaining pantyhose dangle down. Exploring his contorted features under the mask, I notice his hair looks dark, maybe brown, and falls below his ears. His eyes are dark and diabolical. The nylons push his prominent hook-like nose flat. I look closely at his gloves. They appear smooth, almost like sheepskin, and are mustard colored. Obviously, Bevers has learned his lesson about leaving fingerprints. There wouldn't be any this time.

Disrupting my observations, he points to the tub and demands, "Here, get in the tub with this towel and wash off."

I say, "You'll have to help me." As he stands there ignoring me, I implore, "Please help me. My leg's broken. I need help to the tub." Upon his refusal to help me, I hold on to various objects and hobble my way to the tub. Quite awkwardly and painfully, I manage to get into the water. I land with a loud splash that spills more water and blood onto the floor.

Bevers demands I wash all the blood off and roughly shoves my hand back under the water. Knowing the water will make my hand bleed more, but too tired to resist, I submit to his will. The blood begins to flow freely, as he heads back toward Michelle's door.

I sit in the bathtub full with blood and water and watch as Bevers returns to my daughter's door. I keep thinking, You can break my body, but you can't break my mind. But I realize I can't take much more of this monster's physical or psychological abuse. As I am thinking of ways to escape from his clutches, my heart is beating so vigorously from fright that I am again certain it will give out and simply stop beating.

Standing in front of Michelle's door, he looks back at me to be sure I am watching. Grinning and obviously pleased with his ingenious method of psychologically torturing me, he taps his fingertips lightly against my child's door, then starts moving his hand slowly toward the knob. He keeps doing this over and over, sending me almost to the brink of a complete nervous breakdown. I feel that before he broke through my door, he had looked to see which was Michelle's room and if she is home tonight. I shudder, praying she is all right.

Distressed by his behavior, I pull myself out of the tub and flop on the floor like a fish out of water. Startled by the noise, he runs over to the tub, picks me up and dumps me back in. He stoops to get the towel he has dropped beside the tub and dips it in the mixture of blood and water covering the bathroom floor. Using a circular motion, he starts scrubbing the walls with the drenched bloody towel. He eventually moves out of my view, as he works his way toward the living room.

Seizing the opportunity, I get out of the tub once more and land with a loud thud on the floor. I hold my breath. I am in sheer terror that he heard the noise. I lie motionless on the bathroom floor, praying to God Bevers hasn't heard my fall. After I am sure he has not heard me, I slowly start crawling out of the bathroom, dragging the dead weight of my broken leg behind me.

Knowing I will have to divert his attention away from Michelle once I make it to the living room, I crawl until I am sure he sees me, then I slump over, pretending to pass out. Rushing to the linen closet, Bevers appropriates more towels, runs to the tub and soaks them. Wringing the towels out one by one over my body, he attempts to wake me. His frantic attempts to revive me convince me that he wants me to know what is happening until the moment he snuffs out my life.

When he goes to get more water in his quest to rouse me, I amble to my feet, and cautiously hobble toward the kitchen. When I reach the edge of the living room, I spot him out of the corner of my eye as he jumps on me. He flings me against the wall. Satisfied I am not going anywhere, he returns to obsessively wiping objects.

However, unbeknownst to Bevers, when he flung me against the wall, I managed to maintain my balance. I slowly make it to the opposite wall, where my hand touches the ironing board I'd been too tired to put up that night. Careful not to tip it over, I hold on to the board and hop on my left leg until I make it to the kitchen door. I pray Bevers is too preoccupied to notice me. I cringe when I hear him ask, "Where do you think you're going?"

I answer, hoping he'll accept the explanation, "I just want some fresh air, that's all, just some fresh air." The answer seems to appease him, and he proceeds with his ritualistic cleaning.

Standing at the kitchen door, my only avenue of escape, I pray I will make it out as I open the door. I hop into the garage. My heart's cadence is like a drum roll. I manage to take two more steps before he pounces on me like a cat nabbing a mouse.

THE STRUGGLE BY THE CAR is so fierce I twist his watch completely off of his left hand with it ending up on the upper part of my arm. I wrestle free from him, as he grapples with me to reclaim the watch and his control. As he reaches for the gun he had placed in the front of his pants, he grabs me and I'm pushed against the hood of the car. I grasp ahold of the gun as we fight for control of it. The gun discharges as I manage to turn it upward and away from me. I roll off the car's hood when he lets go of me momentarily. The deafening sound of a gun discharging resounds through the garage. The bullet travels through the garage ceiling into the living room, with the spent projectile winding up on the living room couch.

I creep silently, holding on to the car for support, but he locates me in the dark and springs on me again. He hurls me into some bags I have put out for Goodwill. The soft clothing inside cushions my fall. Regaining my balance, I feel my way back to the only focal point in the darkness, the car. I limp to the back of the vehicle and make it to the garage door. As Bevers bends down and starts rubbing the cement floor with the towel he still holds in his hand, I crawl under the garage door, which is raised slightly.

Exhausted, I sit down on a patch of grass to the left of the driveway. Irritated, Bevers hollers at me, wanting to know what I am doing outside, and orders me back in the house. I repeat to him that I only want some air. He gripes, "Look, lady, I won't hurt you anymore, just get back in the house." Too weak to move, I decide to ignore him.

He continues cleaning the floor of the garage and works his way out to the driveway. It appears he is trying to wipe up anything he thinks is blood. Mistaking a grease spot for a pool of blood, he futilely attempts to clean it. While he is concentrating on the spot, I make it to the front porch.

Now outside, I vow he will never get me back in that house. If he is going to kill me, he'll have to do it out here while I scream bloody murder. I pull myself up by the iron gate that had earlier held me prisoner, hoping to hide from him. He notices me and yells, "Nancy, what are you doing?" Trying to sound calm, I repeat my excuse about needing air. Annoyed, he says, "Nancy, you're hurt, get yourself back in the house, clean up, and call an ambulance. Do it now!"

There is no chance in hell I am going back into that house. Outside is my only opportunity of escaping this monster. Taking a deep breath, I firmly reply, "No, I am going to stay here and get air so I can breathe." Defiantly, I sit down on the porch. To my surprise, Bevers returns to diligently cleaning the driveway.

It is now or never. Slowly I lower my body to the ground. On my hands and knees, I begin inching my way across the yard to the neighbors. I balance with my left side, sitting and scooting until I tire, then I alternate and holding the protruding bone— trying to prevent further injury to my leg—scoot some more. I hear him and stop in my tracks. He whispers in an ominous sing-song voice that makes the hairs stand up on the back of my neck, "Nancy, Naaancy…wheeere are youuuu? I'm gonna get ya, Nancy. Naaancy, Naaancy…" His voice rumbles in my ears. My heartbeat accelerates as he repeats the verse over and over. For what seems an eternity, I remain frozen.

When I can no longer hear him, I keep my body close to the ground and resume crawling, hoping he cannot see me in the darkness. Stopping long enough to glance over my shoulder, I cannot believe my eyes as I see a shadow going in the opposite direction. Is he leaving, or am I delusional?

Carefully continuing my journey, I make it to my neighbor's driveway. Crouching down in front of their car, I look back toward my yard and see the taillights of a car parked at the end of Presley Drive. I can barely see in the distance without my glasses. Everything seems a blur, as I concentrate on what the taillights look like. The car starts up, slowly pulls out, then turns right and disappears.

I am in shock, and am not sure if Bevers left. In a stupor, I go back to the task at hand, slowly stealing toward the Schroeders' front porch. My elbows and knees ache and bleed as they scrape the pavement. Advancing toward the door, I reach for the doorbell with my mangled right hand. Remembering what had been done to it, I switch to my left hand, and frantically start ringing the doorbell.

Too weak to stand, I slump part way down on the porch. I notice a hole in the screen. Thank God! My desire to get help outweighs the fear of hurting my hand any worse. I reach through the hole with my right hand and pound on the door. I scream for them to open up and help me.

The Schroeders' five-year-old son, Billy Joe, hears me and cries out to his parents, Vickie and Skip. Skip throws open the front door. He stands frozen as he surveys the vision before him, then pulls me naked and bleeding inside. He does not realize I am his neighbor, until I whisper to him who I am and that I have been raped. I tell Skip that Michelle is still inside the house. He audibly gasps, "My God," then calls out to his wife.

Vickie retrieves a sheet from their bed and compassionately wraps me in it. Skip grabs his gun from the closet and heads for the door. As he is almost out the door, I manage to warn him, "He's got a gun."

Vickie begs her husband to stay with us and call the police. Reluctantly, Skip puts the gun down and reaches for the phone. Vickie wraps her arms around me, gently holding me as she places a brown pillow under my head.

I can hear Billy Joe crying, softly saying, "Mommy, the lady is hurt; she's hurt and bleeding. Oh, she's so hurt."

Vickie calmly tells Billy Joe to go back to bed; Mommy and Daddy will take care of everything.

I look up at Vickie and, feeling safe for the first time, murmur, "Call the police...get Michelle." Exhausted, I lean back into the haven of Vickie's arms.

Chapter 8

The Trauma

I awake to a furor of activity. Although woozy and in a daze, I recognize that I am now lying on the Schroeders' living room floor. A sheet partially covers my battered body.

I hear Skip arguing again, saying he is going to get his gun. Vickie fumbles with the phone directory as she tries to find a number for the police. Unfortunately, 911 does not exist in 1984.

Vickie finds the number and summons the police and an ambulance. I manage to mumble, "What time is it?" Vickie tells me it is a little after 5:00 A.M.

At 5:22 A.M., Officer J. D. Grisham is dispatched to investigate an assault complaint. On arriving, Officer Grisham quickly surveys my condition and ascertains the situation is serious. He immediately calls for back-up and an ambulance.

Grisham and his partner, Sergeant Scott, draw their weapons and slowly approach my house. They do not know what they will find. They thoroughly search the outer premises for a suspect. The officers know I have a daughter and no one is sure if she is in the house or not. Their objective is to find Michelle and then the suspect.

The officers enter my house slowly. They observe that there are blood stains leading to the door that opens from the garage to the kitchen area; the screen on the door is cut; and the small window is open. They follow a trail of blood from the kitchen, through the living room, down the short and narrow hallway into the bloody bathroom, and to the master bedroom. As they carefully walk past the bloody bathroom, they observe water running in both the sink and the bathtub. In the master bedroom they find blood on the floor and all over the bed.

After searching the master bedroom, they turn their attention to Michelle's room. The door is still closed. They have no way of knowing that Michelle has seen their shadows and guns through her bedroom window. She thinks they are there to harm her. As they slowly open Michelle's door, what they see will stay with them for a long time.

Michelle is so stiff, they think she has been murdered. As one of the officers approaches her, Michelle sees he is a policeman and begins screaming hysterically, "I saw and heard it all! Where's my mother? Is my mother alive?" One of the officers assures her that I am alive and have escaped to a neighbor's house. Officer Grisham gently lifts the terrified girl in his arms and carries her out of the house, while his partner makes another cursory search of the premises. Before he leaves, Sergeant Scott turns the faucets off.

Officer Grisham delivers the sobbing, incoherent girl into Vickie's arms and immediately returns to my house to search the premises and surrounding area for the suspect. Although bruised, battered, and in severe pain, I am aware enough to slip my mutilated hand under the sheet and out of Michelle's sight. When Michelle sees I am covered in blood she runs to me distraught and crying, "Are you okay, Mother? Are you okay?" I do my best to look at her in a reassuring manner.

The police notify the Criminal Investigation Division (CID) and secure the crime scene. While I lie on the Schroeder's floor waiting for an ambulance to arrive, I keep mumbling, "He came back. It was the man who raped me before. He said he would come back, and he did!"

Although Michelle could hear a great deal of what happened, she does not know how badly I am hurt. The Emergency Medical Team (EMT) makes sure, as they lift me onto the stretcher, that my right arm and hand stay securely tucked under the sheet.

I am weak and exhausted. Vickie tries to console my daughter. Michelle watches as they load me into the ambulance. I am coherent enough to hear my daughter sob in horror and know there is nothing I can do to help her.

After the EMTs load me into the ambulance, one of them gets a cooler and tells Vickie to fill it with ice. He is going to try to find my severed thumb—in case the doctor can reattach it. As the ambulance driver waits, the EMT runs back to my house and is told by one of the investigating officers that the thumb has been found lying on the bedroom dresser.

The officer warns the EMT that he won't find the whole thumb. They have already tried looking for it. There on the dresser lay my disfigured thumb. The bottom half is missing.

The police overlook the seventeen serrated cuts in the kitchen table top, along with other pertinent and crucial evidence. A friend of mine, Tim Daley, will find the marks later. They were left when the attacker cut up my severed thumb, while I lay unconscious on the kitchen floor. Tim eventually will be responsible for pointing out this evidence to me, and I turn it into the prosecutor on the case.

The EMT quickly picks up the tiny remnant of what is left of my thumb and dumps it into the ice cooler. He runs back toward the ambulance. As he jumps inside, I hear him say, "Let's hit it, boys. Now! Go!"

Chapter 9

The Hospital Stay

I am dizzy. Occasionally, I open my eyes. Strange people run alongside the gurney, blaring lights on the ceiling above their heads. I hear doors slam shut behind me. I am at the same hospital where I was taken after Bevers raped me in 1977.

John Peter Smith, although a county hospital, is a top-notch trauma center. I, luckily, had the presence of mind to request the ambulance attendants bring me here.

As the gurney rolls down the hall, I glance at a clock on the wall. Without my glasses, it is blurry, but appears to read 6:18 A.M.

I hear a nurse say, "Her blood pressure is 128 over 92; pulse is 120. Let's get her into examination room four."

Dr. Mark Presley is the first attending physician to come into my room. He observes several lacerations on my blood-covered head. It is obvious to him I have been severely battered. A bloody mass is attached to my right arm. Upon closer examination the doctor finds a traumatic amputation of the right thumb; a fracture of both the tibia and fibula bones of the right lower leg, with the bone protruding through; and numerous other cuts, abrasions and bruises to the rest of my body. I am only able to sign the consent to treat form with an X.

Despite my repeated pleas for my injuries to be photographed, it is never done.

I am stabilized with IVs in place before the rape exam begins. Talking out loud to the nurse, the doctor notes that there is blood in my vagina with bleeding, swelling and lacerations of the cervix. My anus is swollen and bruised. The vaginal wet mount indicates no presence of sperm; which supports my contention that the attacker never ejaculated.

After the rape exam, I am given a drug to induce spontaneous abortion in the event, God forbid, Bevers has impregnated me. They also give medication to prevent venereal diseases I might have contracted during the assault; however, there is nothing they can give to prevent the newly recognized AIDS virus.

If Bevers is my attacker, and I know he is, he most likely has been assaulted while away in prison. Later I will learn that on top of everything else the rapist did to me, he subjected me to the possible exposure of the deadly AIDS virus. It will be years before I learn I did not contract the deadly disease.

Upon further assessment, the examination reveals two lacerations one-and-a-half centimeters in length over my right frontal skull area; abrasions, multiple bruises, and ligature marks around my neck; abrasions to the face, chest, back, arm, and left knee; and the amputation of the right thumb, leaving only the rough torn edge of my hand, bones protruding, with coagulated blood surrounding the wound. My right leg has multiple abrasions about the knee with a closed fracture of the right lower extremity to the tibia and of the fibula, with the bone protruding out of my leg.

There is no doubt among the personnel, who talk freely about me in the emergency room, that I have put up one hell of a fight to stay alive.

What is left of my thumb had been placed in ice and a saline solution and transported in the ambulance with me. The piece consists of the tip of my thumb. The entire base of the thumb is missing.

I strain to hear bits of conversation as the medical team scurries about the room. I hear enough from the nurses to deduce the tapping sound I heard while lying on the kitchen floor was Bevers whacking at my thumb. I know, too, no one can find the missing part of my thumb. This monster has probably taken it with him, like some kind of a trophy, or worse, devoured it.

I look up and see yet another doctor, Dr. Robert Protzman, a surgeon. He will try to reunite the thumb and hand. The horrible realization of the damage to my hand is absorbed by me when the doctor forces me to view the x-ray. The amputation is at the level of the MCP joint, and the entire proximal phalanx of the right thumb is missing. The EMT who had returned to the scene of the crime to locate the rest of the thumb came up empty-handed. No one can locate the missing part of the thumb.

The cut left by the amputation is quite jagged and goes all the way back to the wrist bone, which also has sustained a deep cut. The doctors concur that it might be possible to reattach the remaining part of the thumb. The plan is to take the distal phalanx and fuse it to the metacarpal region in a functional type position. It is a long shot, but the surgeon decides to give it a try after learning that I am right-handed, a secretary, avid pianist, and organist.

The amputated thumb and I are taken to the operating room. Once there, it is carefully examined under a microscope. They isolate a dorsal vein for venous return and clamp it with a vascular-type clamp. The tip of the thumb is carefully irrigated and is quite dirty. They remove the contaminated soft tissue, skin and bone down to the level of the cartilage of the distal phalanx. They soak the tip of the thumb in an antibiotic solution and then place it in iced saline.

I am given a general anesthetic. Because I have lost an enormous amount of blood, they start a blood transfusion. It will take four pints to replace what I have lost. My right thumb is carefully reattached. They stitch the open wrist wound, cover it with gauze and place a bandage on the right hand. A posterior splint is placed on my right injured leg. It takes eight hours to perform this delicate procedure.

They take me to the Surgical Intensive Care Unit, where I sleep off the effects of the anesthesia. I am in stable condition.

Days and nights seem to run together under the influence of the heavy narcotics I am receiving. At first I am, mercifully, in a drug-induced sleep. I don't know what time it is or even what day, and I don't care.

On September 12, an x-ray of the right lower leg shows that it is crushed in several different places in both the distal tibia and fibula, as well as an oblique splintered fracture at the proximal fibula.

On September 13, I am again in the operating room and under general anesthesia. This time, my right leg is prepped and draped. The skin is closed and a long leg cast is applied. The doctors reevaluate my thumb. It is very black. The surgeon fears that the tip of the thumb is dying. He says it is due to a lack of blood circulation. Dr. Protzman decides to watch the thumb a few more days and give it a chance to survive. I am returned to the recovery room in stable condition.

On September 14, I am back in the operating room. The doctor is checking the status of the reimplantation and elevated pressures in my right lower leg. Dr. Protzman decides more work is necessary on the right leg, so it is prepped and draped. After the operation, my leg is wrapped in a sterile cast and a posterior splint is applied. They remove the bandage from my right thumb and more repair work is done in an effort to save it. Once again, I am taken back to the recovery room in stable condition.

Dr. Protzman consults other staff doctors regarding the deteriorating condition of my thumb. I am told that the doctors have tried valiantly to save my thumb, but all their efforts have failed, mainly because they did not have a clean cut to work with, but rather a jagged and badly butchered hand. It did not help that the majority of the thumb was never found.

I am taken back to the operating room on September 17 for the removal of the previously reattached thumb because of tissue death. After being given anesthesia, my right hand is prepped and draped, and the thumb is removed and sent to pathology. The right leg cast is removed and a long leg cast put in its place.

In a nine-day period, I had four major surgeries. Bevers had done quite a hack job on my hand. On September 24, the doctor did a graft to the right hand. He tells me that later we will discuss the possibility of a prosthesis. I am out of it most of the time. I am given Demerol to alleviate my agonizing pain.

The physical pain is not all I must endure. A couple of days after my admission to the hospital, a hospital security guard comes in my room. He says a man has asked the receptionist if a Nancy Skalias is in the hospital and what her room number is. To protect me, the police made sure I was not registered in the hospital. By the time the receptionist turned around to tell the stranger that no patient was registered with that name, the man had vanished.

The security guard says the police and hospital have arranged to have a guard stationed outside a criminal's room a few doors down and will have him check in on me periodically. Although I am heavily drugged, I know enough to surmise it is Bevers, looking me up to finish me off.

During my stay at the hospital, I receive physical therapy to help me deal with my injuries and the effect they will have on my daily life.

My friends, again, prove invaluable to my recovery. Bill Sanders brings the best medicine available—my daughter. He is one of the first to successfully persuade me to go exploring in a wheelchair. His natural optimism is good for me, and subsequently some does rub off on me.

Carol Nanchy visits regularly and brings little gifts to lift my spirits. One of these is a cute little kupie-like doll with wild, pink hair. I christen my present "my victim doll" and keep it by my bedside. The doll will become my constant companion.

Nancy Heston, a friend who is keeping Michelle during my hospital stay, brings Michelle periodically to see me.

Chapter 10

Betrayal

My first three days revolve around drug-induced sleep, interrupted intermittently by uncontrollable crying. Unfortunately, very little emotional therapy is available.

It seems the police are in as much of a fog as my heavily drug-induced one. While I lie in the hospital, the police call in R. C. Kemp and read him his rights. He is the man I talked to prior to the attack. While R. C. is willing to help the police catch my attacker, he is unknowingly being questioned as a possible suspect; a police artist renders a drawing of him through the two-way mirror/window while he talks with detectives. They let him go with the admonishment not to leave town without notifying them.

They also consider my fiancé, Larry, a suspect, though they never call him in for questioning.

Meanwhile, visitors keep pouring in to see me in the hospital. They are not prepared for my appearance. I am a vision of bruises from head to toe. My head is bandaged where the attacker hit me with the butt of his gun; my leg is in a cast from the many breaks it has suffered; and what is left of my pitiful thumb is a little knob, black as coal, sticking out from a bandage. I look pale and weak. They don't need to say anything; their expressions say it all.

The only thing that seems to cheer me up are the visits from my fiancé, Larry. Even though we have problems, like all couples, I believe our love will overcome any adversities. And so it is in the beginning. Larry is loving, caring, and supportive.

But as I become less medicated and begin to wake up to everyday realities, things take on a different perspective. Each new day I can see changes in Larry. One day, before I am even allowed to get up out of the hospital bed, Larry saunters into my room. He walks over to my bed. As he bends toward me, I ready myself for a soft kiss brushing my lips. Instead, he takes a piece of my hair and flips it against my forehead. He disgustingly and callously asks me why—with the blood still in my hair—I am such an ugly mess. His cruel and uncaring attitude cuts me as sharply as any knife. His visits become less frequent, and when he does come to see me, his attitude makes it clear that it is a chore he'd just as soon not be doing. He just sits in a chair and sullenly stares off in the distance. Not only am I extremely hurt by his treatment of me, I am baffled by his behavior.

After ten days of this treatment, he hits me with the cruelest blow of all…it is over…we are over! The relationship ends because Larry supposedly can't deal with the "pain I have brought on with the tragic rape." He speaks as if this is my fault. Without any real warning, our relationship has gone from looking at wedding rings in July 1984 to ending tersely during a telephone conversation. I cry endlessly. I am in a deep depression. The rapist just keeps taking and taking from me.

Dr. Presley becomes very concerned over my deep depression. The ordeal with Larry has made me hit bottom and I, too, become aware of my fragile mental condition. I beg Dr. Presley to send in a psychiatrist to see me before I descend into a pit of despair out of which I might not be able to climb. I believe I'm on the verge of a complete mental breakdown.

The psychiatrist pays me one short visit, attempting to keep the pieces of the puzzle from falling apart. My doctors encourage me to put on some makeup and get my hair fixed. Their theory: The better I look on the outside, the better I will feel about myself on the inside.

I decide to try their advice, and even have Sukcha, my hairdresser, visit me at the hospital to do my hair. I have a friend bring me a jogging suit and begin to wander out from the confines of my room into other parts of the hospital, but nothing can return all that my attacker has taken.

Chapter 11

Right Place—
Wrong Guy

While my body is being repaired, the rape investigation is being badly botched.

The night of the attack, CID officers search for finger-prints, but find none. The police are not surprised, since Bevers wore work gloves. However, among some shoes by the dresser I had sorted to donate to Goodwill, they find a Zippo-type lighter.

The police are aware that no one in my family smokes, and the lighter is one I have never seen; so, they assume it fell from the attacker's shirt pocket during one of the struggles. Mostly out of procedure, the lighter is dusted for prints. The police believe there will be no prints found because of the gloves worn by the attacker. They are right.

When Detective Bill Martin of the Watauga Department of Public Safety arrives at the scene of the crime, it is turned over to him and he is briefed on what occurred there that terrible night.

Before I am transported to the hospital, Sergeant Scott obtains a physical description of the attacker from me. I tell the sergeant that my attacker was a white male about five-foot-ten, with a slender build; wearing a tan and brown plaid shirt with long sleeves rolled up to the elbows that Larry had given me and had been confiscated from my laundry basket in the garage; blue jeans; brown hair; a wispy moustache; and he wore a stocking over his face.

I also tell the police over and over it is Lanny Bevers, my attacker from 1977. I tell them he had warned he would get even with me if I ever told the police or took him to court. My rapist back then, Lanny Gene Bevers, Jr., fit the physical description to a "T" when I gave it to the police.

Although the stocking over his head had distorted his features, I still recognized the voice, the mannerisms, the face, and his MO (method of operation), which was virtually identical to the 1977 attack.

He is supposed to still be in prison; after all, he had gotten twenty years for the 1977 rape. He cannot possibly be out before 1997. Right? Wrong! Bevers is out on parole, and the board did not even provide me with a simple warning. I learn he has been roaming free and living in close proximity to me for several months.

While the crime scene is searched for evidence, my father, Mr. Kincaid, calls the Watauga Department of Public Safety to advise them that I have told him that a gun was fired in the house. Acting on this information, they conduct a search to try and locate the bullet or casing.

While I lie on the operating table, strange events begin unfolding involving this crime.

The police department is anxious to capture this guy because of the sheer brutality of the attack. Immediately, the officers dispatch an all-points bulletin (APB) of the attacker's description. A police officer with the Watauga Department of Public Safety stops a man in the vicinity of my street for driving erratically. The officer making the stop gets excited when he sees the man he has stopped near my home fits the general description of my attacker.

After Mark Anderson's (a pseudonym) car is stopped, the officer asks him to step out of the car. A routine run on his driver's license shows on the officer's NCIC computer that he has been convicted of a sex crime. The officer reacts quickly, telling Mr. Anderson to place his hands on the top of his car. The officer frisks and handcuffs him, reads him his rights, and places Mr. Anderson under arrest. It seems Mr. Anderson has been convicted of exposing himself to a female student at Tarrant County Junior College, Northeast Campus, approximately five or six miles from the scene of my home. He was sentenced to probation.

As his partner places the prisoner in back of the patrol car, the officer scans the inside of Mr. Anderson's vehicle with his flashlight, revealing the images of naked women on the covers of magazines piled in the back floorboard of the car. He reaches in and takes a closer look. Anderson has a bunch of pornographic magazines in his car.

They impound the car. The police are excited. This has to be the guy. After all, he is a convicted pervert driving around my neighborhood shortly after the rape. They obtain a search warrant for the suspect's house and find women's panties of all sizes crammed in his dresser drawers, under the pillows on his bed, and even in the nightstand beside his bed. Most of the panties are stained with semen. This only solidifies the officers' beliefs that they have my attacker.

Yet, with all this damaging evidence, they still have to contend with my initial outcry and insistence that the rapist of 1977, Lanny Bevers, was my attacker this time, too.

Chapter 12

The Alibi

To bolster their claim that they have the right man, the police must discredit my identification of Bevers as the attacker. With this intent, they dispatch two investigators to Confederate Builders at D/FW Airport, which employs this pain-in-the-ass, Lanny Bevers.

They approach the supervisor, flash their badges and ask him to check the time sheets for a Lanny Gene Bevers, Jr., for the time period of September 7 through September 9, 1984. Their investigation shows that Bevers worked a double shift on September 7 and 8, which means he was working until 3:00 A.M. on September 8.

They learn from questioning the supervisor that Bevers's stepfather—whom he was exceptionally close to—died of a heart attack at home on September 7. The funeral services were at 3:00 P.M. on September 8.

So, Bevers did not complete his last shift. They know that Anderson is the right man; however, because of me, the investigators will have to go to the trouble of accounting for Bevers's time after he clocked out of work. They start the mundane and tedious interviews with Bevers's coworkers. First, they interview coworkers George Carr, Bobby Waggoner, and Jack Martin. Mr. Waggoner says he called Bevers sometime between 4:30 A.M. and 6:30 A.M. on September 8. Carr says he was with Bevers at their work site repairing automobiles until approximately 4:00 A.M.

Two of Bevers's neighbors, Dale Carpenter and Robert Loving, say they saw him at his apartment at approximately 3:45 A.M. Bevers time seems to be accounted for—except for shortly before 4:00 A.M. until a little after 5:00 A.M. No one could pinpoint talking or being with him at that exact time. That left Bevers free to commit the crime somewhere between 4:00 A.M. and 5:00 A.M.

However, the police believe they have the suspect in custody and dismiss Bevers as a potential suspect. It is my contention that Detective Martin believes so strongly in Bevers's innocence, it won't surprise me if he marches Bevers into my hospital room to convince me I am mistaken.

Besides, they don't want to fool with Bevers. He pretty much had an alibi and they have a bigger fish—Anderson, a convicted sex criminal without any alibi during the time the rape took place. It is true that Bevers fit my general description, but then, so did Anderson.

The investigators dismiss my initial outcry that Bevers had returned and decide that Mark Anderson is their man. For all intents and purposes, they close the investigation.

Anxious to get an identification from me, Detective Martin rushes to the hospital with a photograph of Anderson. I am heavily medicated, and am still being given heavy doses of Demerol.

I am in no shape to identify anyone, much less my attacker. Besides, I have told them the name of my attacker. Detective Martin ambles into my room, trying to keep his excitement in check. He is handsome and charming and seems to be a dedicated detective. He calmly says, "La Vonne, we got him! We have an arrest warrant already made out. All you have to do is pick him out. Now, take your time."

I groggily lift my head slowly off the pillow. I feel secure that they have Bevers. With my uninjured hand, I hold the photo spread Martin hands to me. Surprisingly, I see a sketch of my friend, R. C. Kemp, among the group. This angers me, and I let Martin know about my displeasure at seeing a very good friend among the potential attackers.

I search for Bevers's face. I see a man who closely resembles Bevers and who has on a shirt similar to the one Bevers had worn the night of the attack, but there is no picture of Bevers. Confused, I look up at Martin and say, "None of these are Bevers." Martin encourages me to study the photographs closer. I look at the photograph of the only one that even remotely resembles Bevers. The photo is of Anderson. I feel the medication is affecting my judgment. It is certainly lending further to my state of confusion.

Detective Martin presses on, saying, "You gotta recognize him, LaVonne, we know he did it." I can hear the urgency in his voice, but he slightly tempers it with patience. I look closer at the photograph of Anderson, trying hard to study it. My vision is still blurred by the heavy drugs I am being given. My eyes lock in on the shirt Anderson is wearing. It looks just like the shirt Bevers had on the night of the attack.

Tired and groggy, I turn the photograph over and look on the back side. There is the name Mark Anderson. My mind swirls. Maybe Anderson is an alias Bevers is using. Martin keeps saying over and over they have the right man until he convinces me that the picture I hold in my hand is that of my attacker.

So much has happened. I hurt despite the vast amount of pain medication I am taking. I am exhausted. I look again at the photograph of Anderson. He has the same general features as Bevers, especially the hook nose. Maybe the detective knows something I don't, or the photograph simply does not match as easily as I expected. After all, Bevers was masked during the attack, and six years had passed; it is easy to assume his looks have changed.

Still, I can't get rid of the gut feeling that this guy is not Bevers, who I know is my attacker. I ask Detective Martin about Lanny Bevers.

He assures me that I do not need to concern myself with names, just identify the picture. Reluctantly, I point to Anderson's picture saying, "It looks like him." I identify Anderson as my attacker, still thinking in the back of my mind that Bevers is just using the alias of Anderson.

With virtually no physical evidence, no semen to analyze, no fingerprints, all the police have is my identification. Detective Martin leaves seeming satisfied that he has the man in custody who is responsible for the brutal attack on me. Getting in his car, he heads for the office to pick up and execute an arrest warrant for Mark Anderson for Aggravated Sexual Assault with Serious Bodily Injury.

I drift back off into a heavy medicated sleep. The photo lineup just troubles me more. My problems are far from over; in fact, they are just beginning.

Chapter 13

One Tenacious Defense Lawyer

Mark Anderson is booked and charged with the aggravated sexual assault with a deadly weapon of Nancy La Vonne Skalias. Although I have heard he is no choir boy, Anderson has never committed a violent crime. His crimes are just offensive, and somewhat scary. But Anderson has been a thorn in the side of the Watauga Department of Public Safety for a long time, especially after he went out of his way to terrify one couple by peeping in their little boy's room. With no real evidence, the police could only listen sympathetically to the couple's plight.

Finally, they have something to hang on Anderson. They know he is a pervert; it is just the first time he has been so brutal and dangerous.

The smartest move Anderson makes is to hire a local attorney, Tim Evans. After I begin feeling better, I make it my job to find out about this Mr. Evans. I learn he is an extremely intelligent, well-liked and well-respected attorney who plays hardball, but plays it fair. He is tenacious on behalf of his clients, especially when he truly believes in his heart that his client is not guilty of a crime. I soon learn he believes Anderson is innocent. Mr. Evans arranges Anderson's bail.

This might sound funny coming from me, but defense attorneys often get a bad rap. They spend time dealing with the scum of the world, but once in a while, they will get a client who really is innocent of the crime.

Mr. Evans never doubts I was brutally raped. But he does object to the way some of the investigation is being conducted. He makes it known that he feels I made an identification under less than perfect circumstances. He is definitely right about that.

He also makes it known that his client was reared in England and sports a heavy British accent. Mr. Evans reads the report on my attack and knows it would be very difficult for anyone to fake a Texas accent during such a vicious, emotional attack. Almost every day, Tim Evans is after the District Attorney's Office to rethink it's position. But he cannot sway the DA's office, which goes to the grand jury with the case and comes out with an indictment for Aggravated Sexual Assault with a Deadly Weapon against Mark Anderson.

Tim Evans continues to believe in his client's innocence and begins conducting his own investigation. Mr. Evans is the kind of lawyer you would want on your side if you got in trouble, that is for sure.

*A close-up of
La Vonne's
thumbless hand
as it looks today.*

Crucial evidence: The cylinder of the lighter with Bevers's fingerprint. It is the only evidence placing him at the scene of the crime.

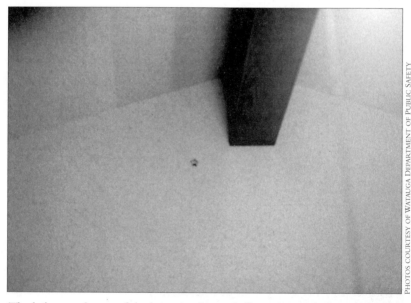

The hole near the top of the beam is where a bullet casing came through. The casing was found laying on the sofa.

Upper portion of garage side of the wall where the bullet hit the ceiling. It traveled through and is found on the sofa.

This is where La Vonne, with a broken leg, her hand and head bleeding, fights with Bevers. Left is the kitchen door; right the hood of her Nova; and on the floor is some of the blood Bevers wiped in circles with a towel.

The shoes La Vonne was sorting to donate to Goodwill. Note near the heel of the red shoes is the lighter.

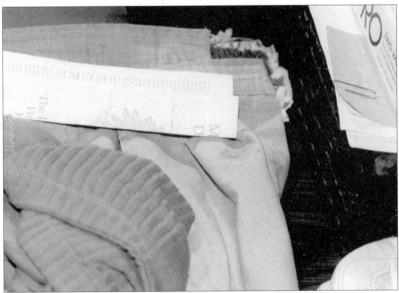

The master bedroom dresser. Police used the paper to point out blood on La Vonne's clothing where tip of thumb was found.

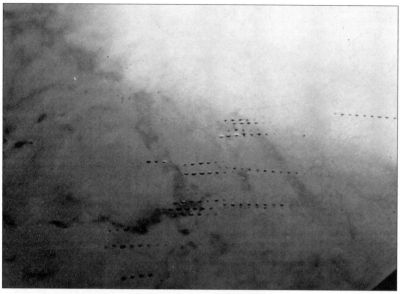

...said to the man who stood at the gate of the year, "Give me a Light that I may tread safely into the unknown" and he replied ~ "Go out into the darkness and put your hand into the hand of GOD, ~ that shall be to you better than a light ~ safer than a known way."

Surface of the kitchen table where Bevers cut up La Vonne's thumb while she lay unconscious on the floor.

The religious plaque Bevers fixated on and wiped in circular motions with a bloody towel. It hung on the wall directly opposite the bathroom.

When La Vonne returns home she learns Bevers had taken a picture of Jesus that was lying on top of the bookshelf and positioned it in an upright position.

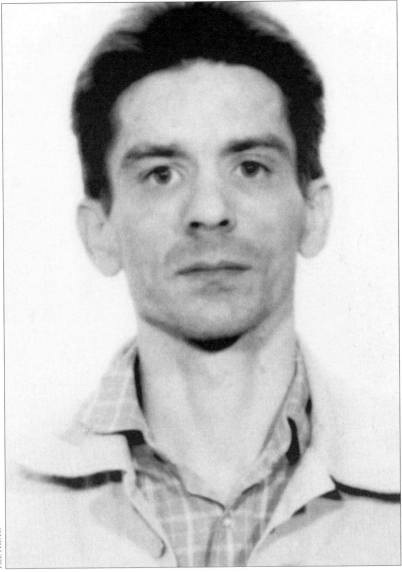

A police photo of Bevers that was taken when he was charged with retaliation.

The hall bathroom where Bevers forced La Vonne into the tub, then taunted her by going to Michelle's door. Note the blood where La Vonne is forced to balance by touching the wall with her mutilated hand.

Bevers shot at La Vonne as she tried to escape. The bullet barely misses her and goes into the mattress.

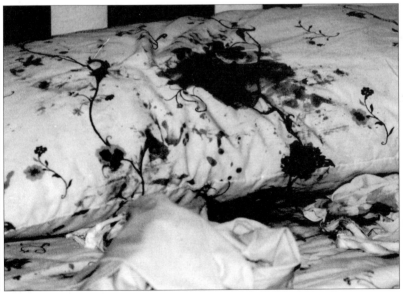

La Vonne's bed, where most of the bloodletting took place. The large amounts of blood on the pillow are from head wounds she sustained (when Bevers twice hit her over the right temple with the butt of a gun) prior to her thumb being severed from her hand

The front door's iron bars blocked her escape. La Vonne bumped into the organ bench trying to escape.

The kitchen. Bevers entered through the door on the left. The table is where he cut up La Vonne's thumb as she was lying on the floor.

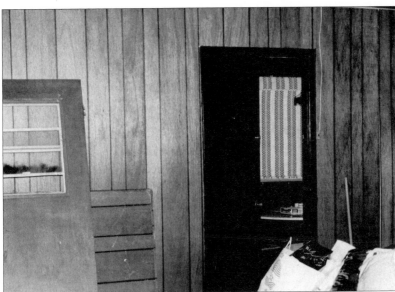

View from the garage to the kitchen. The dark door is new; the old door was taken off its hinges and placed to the left.

Front of the house showing the permanently locked security bars La Vonne had installed after the 1977 rape. In 1984, the bars kept Michelle from escaping through a window from her bedroom, and La Vonne from making it out the front door.

Even after the 1977 rape, La Vonne was opposed to owning a gun. In 1994, she poses with a gun.

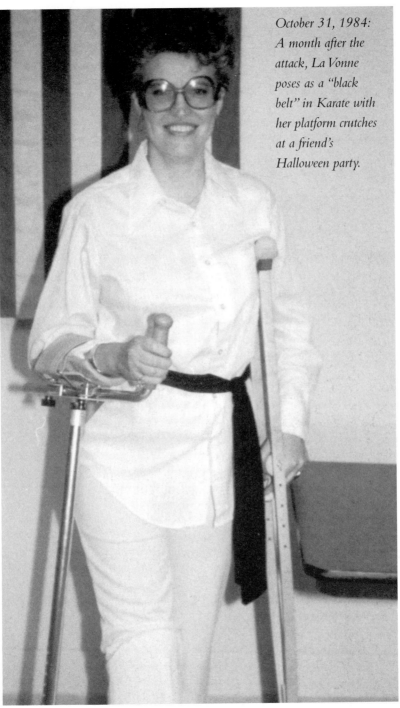

October 31, 1984: A month after the attack, La Vonne poses as a "black belt" in Karate with her platform crutches at a friend's Halloween party.

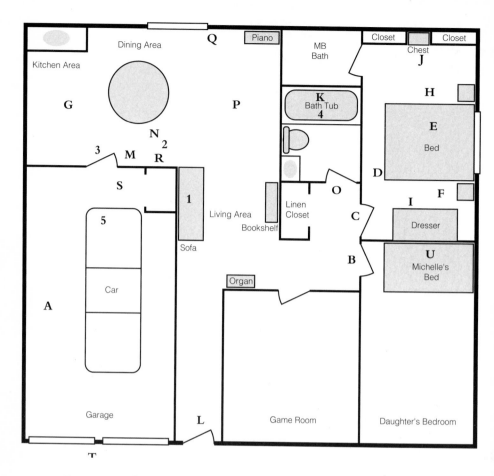

Bevers enters through the right side garage door leaving the door ¹/4 open. The window over La Vonne's bed has bars, and her bedroom door is visible from the outside.

A. Bevers enters through the garage door and breaks into the house through the kitchen door.

B. La Vonne believes Bevers looks in to see which room was Michelle's.

C. He kicks in the master bedroom door.

D. He leaps on La Vonne's bed.

E. He attacks La Vonne as she tries to reach the telephone.

F. La Vonne tries to escape and he shoots at her.

G. La Vonne runs to the kitchen.

H. He catches her and she runs back to the master bedroom phone to use phone.

I He searches through the bedroom drawers.

J. The lighter probably falls out of his pocket at this point.

K. He takes her to the bathtub.

L. La Vonne escapes to the front door, but can't unlock the bars.

M. He catches her, but she escapes and runs to the garage door.

N. He breaks her leg, she passes out, and he cuts up her amputated thumb, then rapes her.

O. They return to the bathroom and he taunts her by opening and closing Michelle's door. He begins wiping up blood.

P. She gets out of tub, goes to the hallway, and pretends to pass out.

Q. He throws her up against the wall.

R. She goes behind the ironing board and out the kitchen door to the garage.

S. They struggle and the gun goes off.

T. She escapes to the driveway and makes it to the front porch.

U. Michelle's bed where she lay frozen with fear as she hears gun shot and her mom's torture.

1. Bullet found on couch

2. Small-length necklace

3. Hair and fiber

4. Longer necklace

5. Hair and fiber

Governor Ann Richards, Governor of Texas, signs an anti-stalking bill which won final legislative approval March 10, 19??.

My father is furious when he finds out my attacker is out on the streets, before I am even out of the hospital. My dad wants to hunt him down and kill him for what he has done to his little girl; not an uncommon reaction for the relatives of victims.

I have found my support once again through Rape Crisis. Only now, Rape Crisis is a huge, professional organization, and very different from the tiny agency I dealt with in 1977. I lean heavily on Jane Bingham, the director of Rape Crisis, for support. Jane is indignant that Mr. Anderson is out on bond. Still, she tries to explain to me and my family that bond is only a means to make sure the person will show up for his court date. At this point, all Jane can offer is advice, comfort, and a strong shoulder for us all to lean on.

In the meantime, I learn Bevers is kicking back and enjoying the fact that he has gotten away with his brutal revenge! Bevers decides he hasn't tormented me enough. He chooses the phone as his next weapon of terror. It will lead to his downfall.

Chapter 14

Terror on the Line

On October 2, almost one month after the brutal attack, I am released to go home. Initially, it is decided that I will continue with physical therapy and use a platform walker. After one week of progressive therapy, I am able to transfer to platform crutches. Within twenty-four hours of my discharge, a home health-care person is found to take care of me.

My fear of going home is so strong I beg Dr. Presley to keep me in the hospital any way he can. Everywhere I turn, fear overwhelms me. However, Dr. Presley has no alternative but to release me and urges my dad to counsel me. Very reluctantly, I return to my house and the same bed I had almost been murdered in. I take with me many open emotional and physical scars.

I have only been in physical therapy a few weeks. Like most, I never gave much thought to how important a limb is in my daily life until I lost one. The frustration of not having a thumb springs up when I least expect it. I have difficulty lifting a glass, eating, and dressing. It seems I did everything with such ease prior to the loss of my thumb. The injury to my leg also proves to be a big problem.

I think about getting a prosthesis for my thumb, but eventually decide to try to get along without one. The rehabilitation to life without a thumb is frustrating, although I am slowly beginning to manage. In learning to do for myself, I have to be creative. I find myself using my teeth, my knees, the crook of my arm, anything as a substitute for the tasks my thumb once so proficiently performed. My left hand takes over and performs tasks that no longer can be performed by my right one. I find new ways to do everything from picking up a glass of water to writing and typing. I feel I am managing this crisis well. Then the telephone calls begin to come.

The calls start the second week of October 1984, only one month after the attack. In the beginning, the caller never speaks, but I can hear the sound of country and western music in the background. It reminds me of the calls I received in 1977. Although Michelle has been through an ordeal, she manages to keep her effervescent personality and attract a lot of friends. My budding teenager is popular with her classmates. Understandably, the phone seems to always be ringing. It seems to be her best friend. I have mixed feelings about it. Her friends are helping pull her out of a deep depression. She is working through the severe trauma she suffered from listening to the rape and not knowing if I would live or die, or if he would come after her next. Nevertheless, the continual ringing of the phone, and her incessant talking on it, are getting on my nerves.

On Monday, October 22, the calls become sinister in nature. Michelle arrives home from school and greets me. I am pleased she is pulling herself back together. My now bubbly, talkative teen answers the familiar ring of her best friend with a cheery hello. Although Michelle's back is to mine, I can sense something is wrong. Really wrong! Turning toward me, the tears trickling down her contorted face transform into hysterical sobs as she slams down the phone.

I can't imagine what happened in one minute to cause Michelle to go from happy to hysterical. Hurrying over to Michelle, I anxiously ask, "What is it? Did something happen to Dad? What is it, Michelle? Tell me what happened."

Michelle manages to stop sobbing long enough to blurt out, "That was him; the man who was in our house."

She had listened to the intruder constantly scream commands at me while she huddled on her bed. There is no doubt the man who just called was the rapist. Wanting to know exactly what he said, I coax my daughter to repeat the words she finds so embarrassing. Between sobs, Michelle awkwardly stumbles over the words. She can't bring herself to use the real words so she substitutes the letters. "He said, 'I'm the man who f—u—c—k'ed your mother, and I'm gonna f—u—c—k you, too.'"

I try to console my daughter. I am consumed with anger. The nerve of this man to call our home after all he has put us through. Reaching for the phone to report the call to the police, I am not sure if I am shaking because I am incensed or frightened. Officer Johnstone arrives shortly and takes the report. He advises me to give him a call if it happens again.

I try to convince Michelle things will be all right. I am grateful for the football season and rigorous school activities, which I hope will keep Michelle's mind occupied.

Things calm down until the first week in November. I am back at work and sitting in for a coworker, Margaret, by manning the switchboard. I notice a pink slip with dates and times jotted down. When she returns, I question Margaret about the slip. Margaret doesn't want to discuss it and tells me to talk to Mr. Dodd, our boss.

I approach Mr. Dodd about the piece of paper and he tells me someone has been calling and saying "F – – – you," then hanging up. Assuring me there is nothing to worry about, he goes on to say it isn't uncommon for high school students to pull such a prank. After all, this is the school administration building. High school kids call all the time saying stuff like that, thinking it is funny.

I am again working at the switchboard, when an obscene call comes through to me. The conversation is so short, I am unable to identify the caller. Wanting to believe Mr. Dodd, I dismiss it as a coincidence.

Michelle and I are advised to keep a log of the phone calls at home. We place a pad and pencil by the phone. On Saturday, December 8, the obscene caller strikes again and shatters our calm day. Michelle answers the phone. The message is short and to the point.

As instructed, I immediately notify the Watauga Department of Public Safety and file a police report. Detective

Martin is notified of the new development. On Tuesday, December 11, Martin brings a tape recorder to the house. He sets up the recorder in the kitchen by the wall phone. A small suction cup attaches to the receiver.

He directs us to continue keeping a log of all incoming calls. As soon as the phone rings, before picking up the phone, we are to push the record button. If it is not the caller, we are to hit the stop button. However, if it is him, we are to continue recording. When the conversation ends, we are to rewind the message and play it back, to make sure it recorded properly.

The two of us try to conduct our lives as usual, but inevitably we both jump anytime the phone rings. The telephone becomes an instrument of terror.

The next call comes on Saturday, December 15, at 3:00 P.M. Michelle pushes the record button and picks up the phone.

Michelle: Hello.

Bevers: Hello, Michelle...(pause)...Michelle?

Michelle: What?

Bevers: Are you ready to give me some pussy?

Michelle: Umm...who is this?

Phone disconnects...

PLEASED THAT SHE HAS CAPTURED the caller's voice on the recorder, Michelle calls out for me to come hear the call. I rush in, and following Detective Martin's instructions, play the tape back. As I listen to the tape with my daughter, I wince at the language. I can deal with the situation, but am not at all happy about my young and innocent daughter being exposed to such filth.

Trying to alleviate the discomfort we both are feeling, I suggest Michelle occupy herself by practicing some school cheers. Earlier, Michelle expressed an interest in trying out for cheerleader as soon as she is old enough. If he calls back, Michelle will be busy and I can take the call, sparing my daughter the unpleasant task of listening to his garbage.

The second call comes a few hours later at 6:00 P.M. I push "Record" and pick up the phone.

La Vonne: Hello.

Bevers: Nancy?…(pause)…Nancy?

La Vonne: Yes.

Bevers: How's your thumb?

La Vonne: Who is this?

Bevers: Nancy? Nancy, listen closely. You want it. You want it, don't you, baby?

La Vonne: What's the matter with you?

Bevers: And, I'm gonna get Michelle…(breathing heavily)…Oh…I'm coming, now, Nancy. Oh, it feels so good. Pretty soon it'll be in your pussy. You want it, don't you, Nancy? Don't you, Nancy? Do you want me to hurt Michelle? Answer me! Yes or no?

La Vonne: I have nothing to say to you.

Bevers: Nancy, do you realize how easy it'd be to sit off with a rifle and shoot the kid? Do you realize how easy it is to burn your house down with you two in it? Do you want me to hurt you two? Do you? Yes or no? It's right at Christmas time, Nancy. I want an answer! Yes or no, or I will hurt both of you, I swear it! Answer me! All right, bitch. You're dead! Good-bye, Nancy.

Phone disconnects…

ALTHOUGH BEVERS WHISPERS through most of the conversation, I recognize his voice. Shaken by his violent tone, I make a mental note of the parts of the conversation that relate to the rape. He called me Nancy, like the rapist; he mentioned my thumb; and he talked about burning down the house. I am more concerned now, because he has become more violent this time on the phone. Our safety is at risk. There is such hatred in his voice. He is getting aggressive, even threatening Michelle. As my hands tremble, I rewind the tape and pray it has properly recorded. It has! Eagerly, I call Detective Martin, who promptly dispatches an officer to collect the tape and leave a new one in its place.

Michelle and I spend a restless weekend trying to pass the time until Monday, when we can temporarily escape this madness. We try to go about business as usual. We do some Christmas shopping and decorate the tree.

I am not in the Christmas spirit, but feel I have to put up a good front for Michelle. It infuriates me this man can continue to disrupt and control my life. Thanks to him, this Christmas will be anything but merry.

We spend a quiet Christmas at my parents' house with everyone pretending nothing is awry. The holiday respite is short-lived. A few days later he calls again. Michelle pushes "Record" as she picks up the phone.

Michelle: Hello.

Bevers: Is your pussy hot? Are you ready to suck my dick?

Michelle: Huh?

Bevers: Is your pussy hot?

Michelle: Huh?

Bevers: Is your pussy hot? Are you ready to suck my dick?
Phone disconnects...

THE NEXT COUPLE OF DAYS, although quiet, are anything but calm. Michelle and I are irritable and seem to be constantly on each other's nerves. The prevailing mood is one of fear and tension.

On Monday, New Year's Eve day, Bevers decides to celebrate the end of the year in his own sick, bizarre way. The calls start at 10:13 A.M. When the phone rings, Michelle pushes the record button, then answers.

Michelle: Hello.

Bevers: ...(long pause)...Hello...(He draws out his words in long sinister whispers)...Miiichhhelllle ...

Michelle: This is not Michelle.

Bevers: Who is this?

Michelle: Sharon.

Bevers: Sharon, I've been watching you. You're going to...(inaudible)...do you want to die? Turn out the lights in the back of the house. Do you want to die? Do you? Good-bye, Michelle. Michelle, I am going to fuck you before you die, and I am going to fuck your mother, and she will die, too, and I will burn your house down. Good-bye, Michelle. Do you want to die?

Phone disconnects...

MICHELLE STOPS THE RECORDER and tries to compose herself before calling me into the room to listen to the call. This is pretty heady stuff for a thirteen-year-old to handle. It is also the longest conversation—and by far the most threatening. I play the tape back twice. The terror in my daughter's eyes distresses me. I will make a point of staying close by the phone today, just in case he calls back.

I select a book off the bookshelf and begin to read. Unable to concentrate, my eyes wander from the text, to the phone on the wall, and back again. The phone rings again at 11:24 A.M. I flinch, put aside my book, and walk into the kitchen. Maybe it is just a friend, I think, trying to placate myself. Taking a deep breath, I push the record button and pick up the phone that now feels like it weighs a ton.

La Vonne: Hello.

Bevers: Did you get a hard dick for Christmas?

La Vonne: What?

Bevers: Do you want a hard dick, baby?

La Vonne: Who is this?

Bevers: I'm the man who's going to fuck you whenever I want you.

La Vonne: What?

Bevers: Turn out the front light and the back light. I'm gonna fuck you, baby. You're gonna beg for it. You want it, Nancy? Michelle sure is pretty. You want me to hurt her? Answer me!...(pause)...Good-bye, Nancy.

Phone disconnects...

I STOP THE RECORDER; my hands are trembling. It makes me sick to my stomach each time this scum-bag utters my daughter's name. Unable to return to the book, I pace nervously back and forth in the living room, replaying the conversation in my mind. He said Michelle is pretty. He has to be following her. Knowing all too well what he is capable of, I grow more agitated and nervous.

At 11:46 A.M., the shrill ring of the phone fills the strained atmosphere. Somehow I know it will be Bevers. Bracing myself, I push "Record" and pick up the phone.

La Vonne: Hello.

Bevers: Hello. Are you ready for me? Michelle sure has gotten pretty. Do you want me to hurt her? Do you?

La Vonne: Why don't you speak in your normal voice, where we can hear you?

Bevers: Why don't you give me some pussy?...(inaudible)...are you...Do you want me to hurt her? Do you? Maybe just cut an eye out, for an example, just to show you I'm not playing. You can't watch her all the time. Do you want to end this? Do you? Answer me, Nancy. I watch you shake your ass every day, baby. You got a nice, tight, little ass. Every day you make my dick hard. But, Michelle's getting a nice, little ass on her, too...(pause)...Okay, Nancy, I guess I'll have to hurt her just to show you. Won't I? Won't I, Nancy? Are you going to answer me, Nancy?

Phone disconnects...

I TURN OFF THE TAPE RECORDER, but I can't turn off the terror inside me. God, this man is sick, a real psycho! I play the tape to be sure it has recorded correctly. "Wait until Martin hears this one," I say out loud.

I grimace when I hear myself ask him to speak in a normal voice "where we can hear you." I pray he hadn't caught the slip of the tongue. He said he saw me every day. Was he watching me at work, too? The thought of him stalking me makes my skin crawl. Of all his remarks, the references to Michelle are the most upsetting to me.

Not satisfied with humiliating, degrading, and mutilating me, he now wants to impose himself on me daily. Bevers preys upon my mind, constantly. I can't stop thinking of him. I can't even begin to try and forget the rape. He will not let me.

I know from my experience with him that he enjoys playing games, and this appears to be one of his favorites. He has mastered the art of utilizing his voice as a tool of terror.

The final call before the new year begins comes shortly after 6:00 P.M. Tired, depressed, and in no mood to celebrate New Year's Eve, I angrily push "Record" and pick up the phone. This time he attempts to speak with a Spanish accent, but he does a bad job.

La Vonne: Hello.

Bevers: Turn your tape recorder off.

La Vonne: What are you talking about?

Bevers: Do you want me to hurt your girl? Do you want me to cut her in the eye or her thumb? Do you? Turn off the tape recorder. I've watched you every day, for a long time, shake your ass. I want some of it. I'm going to give you a choice. Agree to meet me or watch your daughter get hurt. What do you want to do?

La Vonne: Where are you wanting to meet?

Bevers: Where do you want to meet me? It won't take long. All you have to do is pull off your panties and get on your back, and the debt will be canceled. Then, I will leave you alone. Otherwise, she will get hurt. I swear to you that much. Now, what do you want to do? Answer me, now, or I will take it that you want me to use your daughter as an example. Well?

La Vonne: I have nothing to say to you.

Bevers: Very well. When I hurt your daughter you are to blame. You value a piece of your pussy more valuable than your daughter's eyesight. Because I am going to blind her. Do you understand? Do you consider that a fair trade? Do you?...(pause)...Very well, you have made your deal. All you would have had to do was let me fuck you, and I would have left you alone. The bars on your windows, if your house catches on fire, how will you get out? The light in front of the house, the light in back of the house...it does not protect you. I can get there anytime I wish. Now, then, do you wish to reconsider?...(pause) Do you?...(long pause followed by a sigh)...Very well. Good-bye.

Phone disconnects...

PUSHING THE STOP BUTTON, I fight desperately to control my mounting fear. I take notes as I play back the conservation. "Turn your tape recorder off." Damn it, he had caught my earlier slip. He made a reference to my amputated thumb again, too. All his talk about setting fires petrifies me. He is right about the bars preventing our escape in case of a fire. The fire marshal had impressed that upon me when I had them installed. "The debt will be canceled." I puzzle over this remark for a few minutes; it finally occurs to me he means his prison term.

I am indisputably terrified. His threats to maim Michelle and set the house on fire terrify me, just as he intends. Michelle arrives home from school each day to an empty house. The thought he could be hiding to rape and torture my child plays on my mind. Apparently, the rape has not satisfied his reign of tyranny, his lust for revenge. He wants complete control over me, and he damn near has it!

Chapter 15

Call out the Cavalry

am near hysteria when I reach Jane Bingham at Rape Crisis. I tell her about the terrifying calls and want to know why they can't lock this man back up. Jane can tell I am teetering on the brink of a nervous breakdown. She takes down some information and says she will call me back.

Jane is an attractive, petite woman. Although she appears to be delicate and tiny, she is as tough as nails when it comes to protecting rape victims. Almost immediately, Jane calls me back. She tells me after our conversation she was angry and called the DA's office. A telephone recording says the office is closed for the holidays and will reopen on Wednesday. Jane expresses her frustration and tells me she will bide her time waiting for Wednesday to come.

First thing Wednesday morning, Jane calls me to let me know she is about to place a call to the District Attorney's Victim Assistance Office. She is hoping the DA's office or the courts will revoke Anderson's bond and put him back in jail. She also confides in me that she is anxious to see just what the DA's newly created Victim Assistance Office will do.

The Victim Assistance Office had been created to help the victims through the court system. The program's coordinators work with the victims, act as a liaison between the victim and the prosecutor and everyone else in between, accompany victims to court and hold their hands (when necessary), explain the judicial system to them, and help them with anything else that they require. Sometimes, a coordinator is at the courthouse until late at night waiting with the victims for verdicts.

When Jane calls Victim Assistance, it is Barbara Davis who answers the phone. My case is Barbara's first case as a coordinator, and she is nervous. When she hears Jane on the other end of the line, Barbara relaxes. Jane and Barbara are just about the same size, and both possess the tenacity necessary in their line of work. They like each other and have a rapport that exists between people who share common goals.

At the time, little did Barbara know that she would become so involved in this case that it would occupy her for years, take her into a world of terror she didn't know existed, and change her life forever. Before this is over, Barbara and I will become friends.

However, today the job is still new to Barbara Davis, and she is nervous and displaced. One of the back buildings is being fixed to house the new Victim Assistance Unit, but right now she is making do with a borrowed phone and a desk in a tiny corner of the fifth floor DA's office.

Jane's voice sounds urgent. "You've got to help this woman I've been dealing with, Barbara." As Barbara listens to the tale unfold, she can't believe what she is hearing! Progressively, her outrage increases and she becomes infuriated. She is now as angry as Jane is. How dare this jerk call the woman he had raped and gloat over it.

Assuring Jane she will get to work immediately on the problem, Barbara jots down my name and case number. She reads the case file, and is appalled at what the bastard has done to me. She is surprised to discover in my initial outcry, Lanny Bevers is the man I named as my attacker, not Anderson, who has been charged with the crime. Continuing to study the file, Barbara makes a mental note that I have told the police this attacker had raped me in 1977.

Wasting no time, Barbara orders the 1977 case file from the warehouse. When it arrives, she eagerly peruses through the contents. She is confused as to why Lanny Bevers has not been charged with this crime. Barbara writes down my name and telephone number and plans to call me to get more information, and some answers to help her sort this mess out.

When Barbara calls she does not realize that I do not use my first name. "Hello, is this Nancy?" Barbara asks. There is a long pause before I acknowledge I am Nancy. Barbara identifies herself and her reason for calling. I politely tell her I prefer to be called La Vonne. I add that only the rapist calls me Nancy.

Barbara and I click. We have much in common, and share the motto, "At times, I may not win, but I never lose." It is

Barbara who listens to my concerns and tries to do something about them.

Barbara asks me many questions. She promises to do everything in her power to help me. Barbara says she will have the phone company place a tap on my phone. She knows recordings of the phone conversations will not be sufficient to put the caller in jail. We have to prove he is making the calls.

I can't explain why, but for the first time since the beginning of this whole ordeal, I feel I have a relentless advocate on my side, concerned with only me, my safety, and justice. I feel like I finally have someone in the DA's office who will go to bat for me.

Barbara asks Detective Martin to retrieve the tapes in existence and turn them over to her. She, in turn, gives them to the Assistant District Attorney, who has Mr. Anderson's file. He then provides a copy of the tapes to Mr. Evans. Barbara reiterates my feelings on Mr. Evans. She says he is a top-notch attorney who is decent and honest. If the wrong man has been charged with my rape, as Barbara and I firmly believe, she assures me Mr. Evans will right the wrong. She says Anderson was wise to hire Mr. Evans.

The District Attorney requests Anderson's bond be raised and he be placed back in jail. Mr. Evans is furious. He concurs with the DA that the man on the tapes is the rapist. After all, the man on the tapes knows too much about the victim and the attack; however, he argues vehemently there is no way a man involved in such a brutal attack could fake a Texas accent continuously throughout the rape. On the other hand, the man who is on the tapes has used a variety of accents, bad ones, but accents, nevertheless.

Coincidence or not, it doesn't convince the DA to drop the case. Mr. Evans hires a voice expert to analyze Anderson's voice and compare it to the one on the tape; then immediately asks for a physical lineup for his client. He is certain I will not pick Anderson out of a live lineup.

A lineup is arranged, but curiously enough, Bevers has been dismissed as a possible suspect by the police and so manages to escape being placed in the lineup.

Barbara dreads telling me that I will have to pick my attacker out of a live lineup downtown at the Tarrant County Jail. I have been through so much already; I don't need this. But Barbara and I share the same opinion: If Anderson didn't do this, we want him free and the right person charged with the crime, who is Lanny Bevers. However, it seems Barbara and I are the only ones who believe Bevers was my attacker.

There are many times that Barbara tells me she is frustrated with a case. She tells me she tries not to let it get to her. Sometimes, though, she succumbs to what she see as injustice for victims and their pain. She confides in me there are times she closes her office door and cries. She says she can't cry in front of the victims, because she is their strong shoulder to lean on. Days like this, when she has to break the news of the lineup to me, she says she doesn't feel so strong.

The day of the lineup, I am so nervous I can barely walk. From day one, I told anyone who would listen that Lanny Bevers was my attacker; no one believed me, except Barbara. She tells me that my original statement to the police names Bevers as the attacker at least nine times. I had been confused the first time I was told Anderson had been charged with the rape. Whenever I approached Detective Martin to ask what Anderson had to do with Bevers, I was rebuffed and told to let them do their jobs. Kept in the dark, I drew my own conclusion that Anderson must be an alias Bevers used. In my heart, I now know this was not the case. I feel uneasy with the whole situation.

Barbara had promised to accompany another rape victim to court today, so Margaret Ellis, the director of the program, accompanies me to the lineup.

Barbara's sister, Linda Bush, is working as a deputy sheriff's bookkeeper in the Tarrant County Sheriff's Office while all of this is happening. Linda and Barbara are complete opposites in many ways, but with Linda having been a victim of crime, she really knows how I feel. Having heard Barbara talk about the case, Linda knows who I am and introduces herself. Linda also works as a volunteer for Rape Crisis, and, like her little sister, is a big victim's advocate. Linda is so unlike Barbara in many ways, but so much like her in others. For one, they are both on the victim's side, and have many strengths in common. And, they both speak their minds, Linda just a little more graphically than Barbara. But then, Barbara knows my religious background, and Linda doesn't.

Not knowing that Anderson is not my attacker, Linda assures me that they have my attacker. She actually makes me laugh by her colorful language on the treatment my attacker is getting at the hands of the other inmates. She tells me that even criminals have some moral ground. They put rapists, child beaters, and molesters at the bottom of the ladder and treat them badly.

During the lineup, I tell the officer no one looks like my attacker, but I indicate one of the men's eyes are similar to his. He encourages me to mark that individual's box. Under duress, I mark the man I feel most closely resembles Bevers. This misunderstanding will further taint the identification. As I leave, I am confused, frustrated, and on the verge of tears.

During a courtroom break, Barbara hears that things have not gone well at the lineup. Barbara stayed in court until late that day with her victim as they waited on a verdict. When she arrives home around 8:00 P.M., she calls me to find out what has gone wrong.

I say, of course, I did not pick Anderson out as my attacker. Baffled that Bevers was not in the lineup, I became confused and flustered.

We both are understandably upset with the outcome, and neither of us have an explanation as to why Bevers wasn't in that lineup. I didn't feel comfortable marking anyone down as the attacker, and felt like I had been coerced into making a choice. Like most victims, I am still very vulnerable and easily intimidated.

Sensing how troubled I am, Barbara breaks her two cardinal rules: "Don't ever give out your home phone number to victims, and don't bring the office home." She knows I need someone I can rely on day and night. Her sixth sense tells her I will not call unless I really need her. She does not live far from me, and Barbara takes it upon herself to be my guardian angel.

It doesn't take long for Mr. Evans to get a hearing after the lineup fiasco. I was unable to pick his client out, and the voice expert confirmed his suspicions that the voice on the tape was not Anderson. For Anderson, it is all over but the paperwork. Judge Tom Cave signs his dismissal papers. Anderson is shipped back to England. Now no one is charged with my rape.

I am terrified and panic-stricken. Barbara promises me she will forge ahead and not let this case fall by the wayside. Besides, she feels more secure now that she knows I have a tap on my phone. She quickly arranges a meeting with me and Special Crimes Investigators John Hogg and David Whisenhunt. Investigator Hogg is a former Texas Ranger with a rugged face. He exudes a no-nonsense attitude, tempered with an abiding compassion and understanding for victims of crime. Barbara tells me a little about his colorful past dealing with the lowlife criminals of the world, as well as the rich and famous. He had been a major player in one of the most famous murder cases in Texas history, The State of Texas vs. Cullen Davis. Davis, a multimillionaire, was the wealthiest man ever to be charged with a capital murder offense. He had been accused of murdering his stepdaughter and his estranged wife's boyfriend, after receiving an unfavorable ruling in domestic court that day. No matter who the criminal or victim is, or their station in life, Barbara assures me Investigator Hogg does his job with the same amount of dedication and professionalism. Perhaps most important for me is that Investigator Hogg has six daughters and knows how to be sensitive enough to put me at ease with the task at hand.

Investigator Hogg, the director of special crimes, Barbara, Investigator Bob Morris with the District Attorney's Office, Investigator Whisenhunt, Officer Coy Ray from the Sheriff's Department, Detective Martin from the Watauga Department of Public Safety, and I meet to review the case. It is quite a gathering of knowledgeable law enforcement, and for the first time I feel someone is listening to me besides Barbara and my family.

I painstakingly describe the 1977 rape, the 1984 rape, and the calls I have been receiving.

I know Investigator Whisenhunt as a kind, gentle, and soft-spoken man. When I was employed at the municipal court of Fort Worth from 1966 through 1971, he was a young rookie policeman for the Fort Worth Police Department. He was gravely injured in the late sixties when he answered a domestic disturbance call. A man had fired a rifle and the blast had struck Investigator Whisenhunt in his abdomen. His approach is professional, yet sympathetic, and helps relieve much of my initial anxiety as I describe the horrible, embarrassing things that Bevers did to me in the 1984 assault.

We all sit attentively listening as the unnerving tapes of Bevers's threats play. These seasoned investigators, all strong men, are obviously shaken by the invidious tone of the calls. The feeling in the room is mutual: We have to get this son-of-a-bitch before he makes good on his threats.

The tapes end and Investigator Hogg looks over at Detective Martin and asks about the "rope chain" necklace. Could it be traced possibly through a catalog? Detective Martin says he has explored all avenues and has not been able to determine where the necklace was purchased.

Investigator Hogg explains to me that our only hope of getting the attacker is through his continued telephone conversations with me. So far, the calls have been pretty short, with me hanging up on my attacker.

Barbara tells me that she knows by now the phone tap must have led to some suspects, but neither myself nor Barbara have been told the caller's identity.

Investigator Hogg stresses the importance of these phone calls from the attacker since they are our only link to finding him. He instructs me to keep this guy on the phone as long as possible the next time he calls. I am to try and arrange a meeting with him. He assures me they will not jeopardize Michelle's or my safety. I feel comfortable with all but one of his instructions. He told me to go along with Bevers, saying whatever it took to gain his trust, even to the point of seducing him. I voice my concern that a jury will look at any seductive or friendly conversation on my part with disapproval. Everyone reassures me that the jury will be informed up front that the DA's office had requested my help.

In the meantime, the team of investigators work jointly with the phone company to find out where the earlier calls originated. Before we all leave, Investigator Hogg asks me, "Oh, by the way, do any of these names—Lehrman, Blizzard, or Poorman—ring any bells with you?" I answer I don't know of anyone offhand with those names.

Now, all we have to do is wait for Bevers to take the bait. It will be a while.

Chapter 16

The Trap

Three weeks pass before I hear again from Bevers. On Saturday, January 19, 1985, the phone rings. It is 6:51 P.M. Once, each time the phone rang, we worried it would be Bevers; now, our greatest fear is that it isn't him. The rape investigation has been so badly bungled, this is our one shot at getting him locked up.

Michelle prays it is Bevers as she pushes "Record."

Michelle: Hello.

Bevers: Hello, Michelle,

Michelle: Who's this?

Bevers: I'm the one that's going to fuck you. Are you ready? Huh?

Conversation ends...

HE HAD TAKEN THE BAIT. Michelle hollers for me. Enthusiastically, I rewind the tape to play it back. It has not completely finished playing when the phone rings. In my confusion, I push the record button, not realizing it will record over a portion of the previous conversation. Eager to try out my rehearsed lines, I pick up the phone. This time Bevers attempts a new accent. Like the other accents, he can't seem to pull it off.

La Vonne: Hello.

Bevers: Hello, Nancy? How are you? I'm sorry I had to leave for a while. But, since they found that bitch, Heller, I had to leave town. It's cold tonight…(long pause)…There…I just came…(heavy breathing)…In a little while I will cum (sic) in your pussy, pretty soon, huh? Do you like that?

La Vonne: Why don't you just leave us alone?

Bevers: Why don't you just give me some pussy? Then I will leave you and your daughter alone.

La Vonne: And how can I do that?

Bevers: Think. You are a bright woman.

La Vonne: Well, what are you wanting?

Bevers: Pardon?

La Vonne: What are you wanting to do…I mean, where are you wanting to…

Bevers: I just want to make love to you.

La Vonne: Where?

Bevers: Where would you like to meet?

La Vonne: You want me to meet you?

Bevers: Yes.

La Vonne: Where?

Bevers: Your house would be fine. But I do not want to make you feel threatened. I do not wish to hurt you.

La Vonne: Don't you think it would be better to meet someplace else first?

Bevers: I do not have the time.

La Vonne: I would think it would be better to sit down over a cup of coffee. Discuss it or something, you know.

Bevers: We can discuss it now. I do not wish to hurt you. Understand this.

La Vonne: You've already hurt me.

Bevers: I have? How have I hurt you? Tell me. Please. I do not wish to harm you.

La Vonne: Well, who are you?

Bevers: A man who wants you very much. You should feel honored. Now, how do we resolve this problem?

La Vonne: Where did you go out of town?

Bevers: This is not your concern. Turn off the back porch light...the light you have on the roof. Unlock the door and leave it unlocked for tonight, and we will resolve this problem. Perhaps you will enjoy it, and we can make it a regular affair. Does this not please you?

La Vonne: I don't understand you. I don't know why you're doing this.

Bevers: Because I wish to make love to you. Is that so difficult to understand?

La Vonne: Like you did before?

Bevers: I am sorry. I do not understand.

La Vonne: Then, why are you calling here?

Bevers: Because, I wish to join with you. You seem to be a

reasonable person. So do as I ask.

La Vonne: Where do you know me from?

Bevers: Goodnight, Nancy. I will see you later. It's cold.

La Vonne: Uh, why can't you answer me? Where do you know me from?

Phone disconnects...

BEVERS, I LATER LEARNED, placed these two phone calls from his father-in-law, Robert Poorman's house. I feel awkward trying to converse with the man who had brutally attacked me, but I am proud I have been able to keep him talking. I feel empowered by the control I am regaining over my life. He appears to believe I want to rendezvous with him. I am disappointed that I have been unable to get him to confess his crime; nevertheless, I feel good about the way things have gone.

Detective Martin, although he knows he should have listened to me instead of ignoring my pleas that Bevers was my attacker, cannot bring himself to look me in the eye and say, "I'm sorry I didn't pay more attention to you." However, he makes a colossal effort to cooperate and help get Bevers on the assault. What he doesn't know is how much I need him to validate my feelings by apologizing to me for not paying attention from the beginning.

When I call and tell him Bevers wants to meet with me, Detective Martin immediately comes to my house. Officers with walkie-talkies are strategically placed in unmarked cars along the street. Everything seems surrealistic, like I am watching a suspense thriller. Except this drama is real, and I'm smack-dab in the middle of it all—the unfortunate central character.

Tension saturates the air as Detective Martin sits with his .45 magnum trained on my unlocked door. Everyone wants it as easy as possible for Bevers to step into their deadly trap. If Bevers calls back, I am instructed to try and get him to meet me at the house tonight. When the call comes, I am unable to record it. Spending the night in Michelle's room, I am apprehensive about running through the living room to grab the kitchen phone. This was something we had not thought about. The last thing I want to do is startle Detective Martin and be the recipient of a well-intentioned but misguided bullet. During our unrecorded conversation, I am successful in convincing Bevers to come over. He instructs me to have all the lights off, unlock the door, and to undress and wait for him.

Detective Martin has me turn on the light in the master bedroom. Nervous and uptight, I flip the light switch. As the light bulb pops and flickers out, I almost jump out of my skin. With the light burned out in the bedroom, I turn on the light in the bathroom across from Michelle's room. Detective Martin props my bedroom door slightly open with a green suitcase, allowing a soft light to shine outside the bedroom window.

Waiting for Bevers to arrive, I keep looking out into the living room for reassurance Detective Martin is still there. I am certain he can hear my heart pounding. Hearing a noise outside, I tiptoe to the window and carefully peek out. I observe a dark-colored car slow down, then speed up as it passes the house. Four times the car turns around at the stop sign and repeats its pass in front of the house.

It is now in the early morning hours of Sunday, January 20. It has been approximately ten minutes since the car passed by the house. The phone rings. I answer the phone in Michelle's room. Bevers sounds upset, saying, "Nancy, you do not want to make love with me tonight. There is a light on in your bathroom. I saw the light from the bedroom window." I assure him the light is harmless, and I am waiting for him. I reiterate all his instructions have been carefully followed. He warns me there better not be any police and wants to know why he has seen unfamiliar cars on the street. I explain to him that a neighbor boy across the street just came home from the hospital. Some friends are staying over to help take care of him.

Ten minutes after we finish talking, I see the dark car return. It passes by the house twice before leaving. A half an hour later the phone rings.

Bevers sounds agitated, saying, "Nancy, you do not wish to make love with me tonight."

I tell him I don't understand what he is talking about. He tells me he has been by the house and has seen the police in the field with walkie-talkies; unmarked police cars on the street; and a cop in the house. The thought that I might jeopardize his safety upsets him. He begins to ramble. He tells me he knows intimate things about me and says he will come over some other night. I hang up displeased. I want this nightmare to end tonight.

I don't know if he really spotted the police or if he is just testing me. It disgusts me to try to talk my rapist into coming over and making love to me. It makes me feel filthy and worthless.

To be on the safe side, Detective Martin keeps vigil in my living room the rest of the night. Now that the trap has been set, it is too dangerous to leave me without police protection. An officer will be stationed at my house at all times.

A team of special agents is sent to stake out Lanny Bevers's job and home. No one wants to see this man walk away scot-free from this crime! We are all anxious to catch him before he hurts me or anyone else.

Over the next few days, I go through the motions of my normal activities, but my mind is always on catching Bevers and ending this nightmare.

It is Wednesday, January 23, before he calls again. It is 11:10 P.M. I am able to record this call. Bevers reverts to his poor Spanish accent as he speaks:

La Vonne: Hello…(pause)…Hello.

Bevers: …(inaudible) …

La Vonne: Hello.

Bevers: …(inaudible)…

La Vonne: I can't hear you…I…

Bevers: How are you?

La Vonne: I can't hear you.

Bevers: …(inaudible)…have you?

La Vonne: Yes.

Bevers: …(inaudible)…

La Vonne: Yes…(inaudible)…I'm doing all right. I thought you were coming…

Bevers: Oh, Nancy, you tried to trap me.

La Vonne: No, I didn't.

Bevers: Yes, you did. You made me very angry. I had to stop. I had to calm down. I did not want to hurt you, so I had to stop.

La Vonne: Well, I want you to think about something
…(inaudible) came here the first time, you hurt me, and I have
to be sure that you won't hurt me again. That you'll come and
maybe we can be friends and, like you said, turn it into an affair.

Bevers: You tried to hurt me when you tried to trap me,
Nancy.

La Vonne: No.

Bevers: You tried to trap me.

La Vonne: No, I didn't. I did just as you said, and I had to
get my daughter elsewhere so I could be here alone. I had the
lights out. I did everything I could. I thought you wanted to
make love to me.

Bevers: I do.

La Vonne: You do?

Bevers: Yes. Are you ready for me to make love to you,
Nancy?

La Vonne: Yes.

Bevers: We will have to work something out. I will have to
think about this, cause I still think you tried to trap me.

La Vonne: No. No. I promise you, uh-uh. No, everything
was just fine…just as you had said.

Bevers: Who was that I saw in the house?

La Vonne: Who did you see in the house? I don't know. I
was here. I was here waiting for you, and I did just as you said. I
kept up my end of the bargain.

Bevers: Nancy, did you realize that if it were a trap that
someone would get hurt?

La Vonne: I didn't have anything to do with any trap. I
don't know what you're saying to me.

Bevers: Okay. I believe you.

La Vonne: Well, please do, because I don't know anything about any trap.

Bevers: Okay. I believe you. Very well, we're going to be friends. Talk to me.

La Vonne: Well, we could be friends, if you just won't hurt me again. I know that first time you hurt me, and I don't want you to do that. You got to promise me not to hurt me. Don't you see that leaves me with a dilemma?

Bevers: That is up to you, Nancy, as to whether or not I hurt you. I do not wish to hurt you, and I do not wish to be trapped.

La Vonne: Well, I don't see how you would be trapped, if I'm here alone.

Bevers: If you are alone, there will be no trap, and you will not be hurt. It is agreed.

La Vonne: It is agreed, and it was agreed then, too.

Bevers: Very well.

La Vonne: Are you going to come see me?

Bevers: Tonight?

La Vonne: Uh-huh.

Bevers: No, not tonight.

La Vonne: Why?

Bevers: There are other things to do. I would like to, though. You looked very good today.

La Vonne: I looked good today?

Bevers: Yes.

La Vonne: What did you like about me today?

Bevers: I like you every time I see you. You are a very pretty woman.

La Vonne: If I am pretty, why did you cut my thumb off?

Bevers: I didn't do this thing.

La Vonne: But, that's what I'm afraid of you for. You did this before.

Bevers: I did not do this thing. I never do… (inaudible)…Why would you think I would do such a thing?

La Vonne: Well, you knew my thumb was off.

Bevers: This I do know. Did they fix it?

La Vonne: Well, you should know if you see me every day.

Bevers: Did they fix it to your satisfaction? Do you play the piano, still?

La Vonne: Do I still play the piano?

Bevers: Yes.

La Vonne: Yes.

Bevers: Good. How is your daughter?

La Vonne: She's fine.

Bevers: Good. This is good.

La Vonne: Does that make you feel good?

Bevers: Yes.

La Vonne: How long have you known me?

Bevers: A while.

La Vonne: A while? I wish I could see you tonight.

Bevers: For what reason, Nancy?

La Vonne: I'd just like to talk to you. Sit down and talk to you.

Bevers: You may talk to me now.

La Vonne: But, I'd like to look at you and talk to you… know…know what you're like.

Bevers: Perhaps we will arrange it.

La Vonne: I tried to tell you, maybe it would be easier if we met in a public place, where there's lots of people and where you'd feel comfortable, and I'd feel comfortable and, uh, you know, have coffee.

Bevers: No. First, Nancy, you must show me that you wish to make love to me.

La Vonne: Now, how can I do that?

Bevers: There will be a time. You do like to make love?

La Vonne: Do I?

Bevers: Yes.

La Vonne: It's a lovely thing.

Bevers: Then, I look forward to it.

La Vonne: Do you love me?

Bevers: Do I love you? I do not know you good enough. I think you are a very fine person.

La Vonne: Then why don't you meet me in a regular way and…I don't understand.

Bevers: It will all become clear in time.

La Vonne: I will eventually understand?

Bevers: Yes, yes, you will understand.

La Vonne: You promise me that?

Bevers: Yes, I promise.

La Vonne: And without harming me?

Bevers: If you do not make me harm you, I will never harm you. I do not wish to hurt you or your daughter. If you will. . .

La Vonne: Well, how do you know about my thumb?

Bevers: Pardon me?

La Vonne: How did you know about my thumb?

Bevers: I cannot tell you this, at this time, but I know many things about you. Things that you think no one knows. This, perhaps, because I know these things, is why I'm attracted to you.

La Vonne: Yes, well what is this thing...this special thing?

Bevers: There are all kinds of special things. Do you wish me to come tonight?

La Vonne: Yes.

Bevers: Is your daughter at home?

La Vonne: I can make arrangements.

Bevers: No. It would not be fair to wake her up.

La Vonne: Perhaps, just let her stay asleep.

Bevers: Perhaps.

La Vonne: Do you think that would work?

Bevers: It would perhaps work. If you would not make me hurt you or your daughter, because I do not wish to do this.

La Vonne: If I don't make you hurt me or my daughter?

Bevers: Yes. I just wish to make love to you.

La Vonne: Just to make love to me?

Bevers: Do you not wish this?

La Vonne: Yes. I'm anxious to meet you. I want to know what you're like. I don't, you know, understand all the things you're saying...these special things about me, and maybe you could tell me.

Bevers: Just know that you are a very special person. Does that not make you feel . . .

La Vonne: That I'm a special person, that makes everyone feel...(inaudible)...to make everyone feel they're special, doesn't it? I would think so.

Bevers: Well, good, because it is true. You are a special person.

La Vonne: Aren't you a special person, too?

Bevers: Perhaps, in my own way. I must go now. It will not be tonight, but soon.

La Vonne: Oh, I thought you were coming tonight.

Bevers: No, but soon. Sleep good. Sleep well. Goodnight.

La Vonne: Goodnight.

Phone disconnects...

EVERYONE AGREES, I have done an excellent job. I consider it strange how his language changes and he uses odd phrases like, "I didn't do this thing." Although I still can't get him to admit hurting me, he had mentioned the piano, another link to the rape. I will do whatever is necessary to apprehend Bevers.

The next call comes on Thursday, January 24, around 1:00 A.M. Apparently feeling comfortable with the Spanish accent, he uses it again, but this time he whispers:

La Vonne: Hello.

Bevers: Wake up, Nancy! Do not go to sleep yet.

La Vonne: What?

Bevers: Do not go to sleep yet.

La Vonne: What?

Bevers: Listen to me!

La Vonne: Okay.

Bevers: I wish to come. I wish you to talk to me while I do so. Talk to me and make me come. Prove that you wish to be my woman.

La Vonne: Right now?

Bevers: Now.

La Vonne: Why don't you come see me?

Bevers: I cannot right now. I wish you to tell me what you wish to do to me. I wish you to tell me...I wish you to talk to me so I can come, now.

La Vonne: ...(inaudible)...

Bevers: Talk to me, now!

La Vonne: Well, I'd like for you to kiss me and hold me and make me feel good and you feel good and...

Bevers: You are in bed...what do you have on?

La Vonne: A nightgown.

Bevers: A nightgown? What does it look like?

La Vonne: It's silk and it has lace on it.

Bevers: Pull it up. Do you masturbate, Nancy?

La Vonne: Sometimes.

Bevers: Masturbate right now when you talk to me. I wish for you to. Do you like oral sex, Nancy? Do you like to perform oral sex? Talk to me and tell me.

La Vonne: Yes. Do you like that?

Bevers: Yes, Nancy. Talk to me.

La Vonne: You like that...you like oral sex?

Bevers: Yes, Nancy. Do you like to have oral sex on you?

La Vonne: Yes.

Bevers: Would you let me do it on you?

La Vonne: It's better that you come here and do that personally.

Bevers: I will, Nancy. I will. Talk to me, Nancy.

La Vonne: Why don't you come tonight?

Bevers: I cannot. I have something I must do. I would like to be there with you, holding you.

La Vonne: Well, what is more important?

Bevers: There is something that must be done, that is very serious. Someone has made a bad mistake. I must fix this. People cannot do these things to me. I must show them this.

La Vonne: Oh, who would want to hurt you?

Bevers: Do not deviate from the subject. Talk to me and make me come, now!

La Vonne: I know, but if you were holding me, wouldn't it be better?

Bevers: Yes, it would.

La Vonne: And it would make you feel better.

Bevers: Yes, but these people must pay for this, and they will tonight. I promise!

La Vonne: Oh, don't go get yourself into problems.

Bevers: There will be no problems for me. Do you understand?

Part of the conversation cut off—tape is being turned over.

La Vonne: You do want me to?

Bevers: Yes. I wish you to.

La Vonne: It feels good. It's hard with the phone, though. It would be better if you were holding me. Don't you think?

Bevers: I think so.

La Vonne: This way is not very good. It would be so much better if you were holding me. I'd just rather, you know, know that you were here. It makes things feel better, don't you think?

Bevers: Yes, it does.

La Vonne: It's not good to be apart. It's better to be together...have you touch me in special ways.

Bevers: It will not be long.

La Vonne: You said you want me to be your woman. Is that correct?

Bevers: That is true.

La Vonne: And you don't wish me any harm?

Bevers: That is true.

La Vonne: Well, I wish you would come on tonight.

Bevers: What color are your panties?

La Vonne: They're white.

Bevers: Pull them off.

La Vonne: Right now?

Bevers: Right now.

La Vonne: Okay, just a minute...uh...(pause)...there ..

Bevers: Lay back on the bed.

La Vonne: Okay.

Bevers: Are you comfortable?

La Vonne: Yes.

Bevers: Open your legs, Nancy...(pause)...wider.

La Vonne: Okay.

Bevers: Close your eyes. Think pleasant thoughts. Let your fingers drift to the good spots. Do you like it, Nancy?

La Vonne: Yes, but you'd be better.

Bevers: I will be there before too long.

La Vonne: Tonight?

Bevers: Not tonight.

La Vonne: This would be better than your going and taking care of other things, that are not more important.

Bevers: These people must pay, tonight!

La Vonne: Why? I'm more important.

Bevers: You are, but these people must pay. They will die! This I swear!

La Vonne: Oh, but . . .

Bevers: That is enough. You have done what I asked.

La Vonne: Oh, but, I don't want you to do that. I'd rather you come here and make love to me.

Bevers: This is all, Nancy. Goodnight. I will talk to you later.

La Vonne: Please don't go yet.

Bevers: Make yourself come, Nancy, and you should feel better. Think of me...think of me between your legs. Think of me holding you, kissing you, caressing you, making you feel like the woman you are. Think of that, Nancy.

La Vonne: I will.

Bevers: Goodnight, Nancy.

La Vonne: I'd rather you come here.

Bevers: I wish to come. I wish to come inside of you.

La Vonne: That would be nice. You like that, don't you?

Bevers: Yes, I do...(inaudible)...I wish to come in you very much. Before long.

La Vonne: How much longer?

Bevers: Before long. Goodnight, Nancy.

La Vonne: Tomorrow?

Bevers: Goodnight, Nancy.

Phone disconnects...

DISAPPOINTMENT SWEEPS OVER ME as I hang up the phone. We won't see Bevers tonight. I am disturbed by his threats that "people must die." What poor, unsuspecting soul might encounter his wrath tonight? Although the police are watching the house, they do not always have someone spend the night in the house. Therefore, my cousin, Linda, arranged earlier to sneak a friend, Rick Wyatt, into my house to spend the night, just as a precaution. I feel more at ease with his presence.

The conversation embarrasses me and I dread the day twelve jurors will listen to it. Will they be judgmental? Will I look like a harlot? Will the defense attorney use my own words against me? Even though Investigator Hogg and Barbara constantly reassure me the jury will be instructed that the DA's office had solicited my help, I still worry.

Barbara tells me her admiration for me mounts as she transcribes this particular tape. She feels it takes tremendous strength and courage on my part to calmly discuss oral sex with Bevers after what he did to me.

Barbara feels my sense of humor is an invaluable asset in helping me to survive. For instance, we laugh when we consider that when Bevers inquired about the color of my panties, I had blurted out white. There I was trying to seduce a degenerate and couldn't come up with more appropriate colors like red or black. It is either laugh or cry.

One call is traced to Bevers's place of employment on White Settlement Road in Fort Worth. The jerk is making obscene phone calls on company time. Watauga Department of Public Safety Investigator Johnstone, Detective Martin, District Attorney Investigators Coy Ray and Bob Morris, and DPS agents Jack Morton and Kenneth Henson are the surveillance teams responsible for watching Bevers's job site and his stepfather's residence, the two places from which Bevers has an affinity for making calls.

Bevers has to be trapped at his own game. His ego is about to let the cat and mouse game go too far, and this time he will be the one who is trapped.

On Friday, January 25, I have what will be my final conversation with Bevers. Undercover Officer John Gibbs (pseudonym) is stationed in the house with his walkie-talkie. That night, the stake-out team follows Bevers to work. They position themselves with walkie-talkies and binoculars so they can catch him in the act of making a phone call to me.

Everyone feels victory is close at hand. Officer Gibbs is to notify the surveillance team by walkie-talkie whenever my phone rings. They will observe Bevers to see if he is using the phone at the same time. Unable to rest, I am thankful tomorrow is not a work day. I pray this nightmare will soon be over.

When the phone finally rings it is 12:29 A.M. I have fallen into a deep sleep. I am disorientated and groggy. Officer Gibbs signals on his walkie-talkie to the stake-out team a call is coming in. They train their binoculars on Bevers. I push the record button, and try to awaken. Bevers's previous call had been mellow and polite, even romantic. This time he begins talking in a calm, friendly tone, but grows more hostile as the conversation progresses. I am relieved to have a police officer with a gun nearby. This will be the last conversation I will ever have with Bevers—the last time I will ever have to listen to his voice!

La Vonne: Hello.

Bevers: Nancy, it's not so good to sleep so hard.

LaVonne: I can't help it. I'm tired.

Bevers: Why are you so tired, my darling?

LaVonne: …(inaudible) …

Bevers: Why?

LaVonne: …(inaudible) …

Bevers: Talk to me and tell me.

LaVonne: All right. I don't know.

Bevers: Why do you have your bedroom door closed?

LaVonne: Why do I have it closed?

Bevers: Yes.

LaVonne: …(inaudible)…

Bevers: I see. You should go to bed earlier.

LaVonne: Well…I just don't know.

Bevers: Did you have a hard day today?

LaVonne: Oh, I guess.

Bevers: I see. I am sorry for this. You should not work so hard. It is not good that you are tired.

LaVonne: Well, did you get your problems taken care of today?

Bevers: Most of them, yes. Most of them, yes. It was good. It went good.

LaVonne: So, you took care of what it was you were going to take care of?

Bevers: Yes.

LaVonne: And you feel good about it?

Bevers: I feel satisfied.

LaVonne: …(inaudible)…

Bevers: Yes. But enough of my problems. Tell me yours. Do you have problems?

La Vonne: Doesn't everyone? I think when you're in life, you've got problems.

Bevers: What are your problems, Nancy?

La Vonne: I don't know...sometimes I just get tired. Don't you?

Bevers: I believe everyone gets tired.

La Vonne: ...(inaudible)...one day, maybe. I just wondered how things have gone for you. You had, you know, me somewhat concerned.

Bevers: I take care of my problems. I always have. I always will. I do not need any help, but thank you for your concern.

La Vonne: Well, you had stated that there was someone, I think, that was troubling you, yesterday, and . . .

Bevers: They will no longer trouble me.

La Vonne: They will no longer trouble you? Well, I just did not know if you were still, uh, you know, into a situation there. So what was bothering you yesterday is gone?

Bevers: Yes, this is true. I did not mean to wake you, but I was curious.

La Vonne: Why my bedroom door is closed?

Bevers: Yes.

La Vonne: How would you know my bedroom door is closed? I don't understand how you know.

Bevers: It was easy. I know where your bedroom window is that looks on to your bedroom door. Tonight I could have come in if I wished. But I do not wish to frighten you. I do not wish to scare you. That is the reason we have these conversations, so that you may be at ease. I do not wish to hurt you. I do not wish to frighten you. If I had, I would be there now.

Especially as hard as you sleep. It is not good to sleep so hard sometimes.

La Vonne: No, but sometimes when I'm tired, I sleep harder than others.

Bevers: This is true. But do not worry. No one will bother you. I will make sure.

La Vonne: Didn't you tell me the other day that you had been gone out of town?

Bevers: Yes. I had some business to take care of.

La Vonne: But, I thought you said it was because of . . .

Bevers: This is not your concern.

La Vonne: I was just worried. I wondered if, you know...

Bevers: Do not concern yourself. I must go. You go back to sleep.

La Vonne: Well, I wondered why you didn't come to see me.

Bevers: I was there, but you did not see me. Had I wished, I would be there with you now. Between your legs, where I belong. However, I wish for you to invite me there, not for me to take you. I do not wish to rape you. I do not wish to fuck you. I wish to make love to you. There is a difference. Do you understand?

La Vonne: Yes.

Bevers: Do you understand the difference between rape. . .

La Vonne: Yes.

Bevers: Do you, Nancy? Or, are you a bitch? I do not wish for you to be a bitch. There are enough bitches in the world. If you are a bitch, I will fuck you hard, and I will hurt you. If I have to rape you, I will hurt you even more. Do you understand?

La Vonne: Yes.

Bevers: Is such a thing worth being hurt for?

La Vonne: No.

Bevers: Is it?

La Vonne: No...like you hurt me before?

Bevers: You have been hurt before. This I know. But, was it worth being hurt for?

La Vonne: But, you were the one who hurt me before, right?

Bevers: No. I was not. I would not do such a thing unless you forced me to. I have hurt people before, but not you, Nancy.

La Vonne: Did I force you to hurt me?

Bevers: I have not hurt you. I have hurt many people before, but never you. Do you understand?

La Vonne: ...(inauible)...

Bevers: Sometimes, they try. Do you understand the difference now, Nancy?

La Vonne: I'm trying to understand a little bit better. I think I do.

Bevers: Tell me, Nancy, what about...(inaudible)...that is true. The strong will always take what they wish. Nancy, I wish you, and I am strong. You must resign yourself to this fate. It is the way it is, the way it will be. When the time comes, do not fight, but give yourself willingly. Do you understand?

La Vonne: Well, you don't use force if you're...

Bevers: I should not have to. Do you wish to give yourself to me, Nancy?

La Vonne: Yes.

Bevers: Then, fine. There will be no problems between you and I.

La Vonne: I will give myself to you if you won't, you know, threaten me with a weapon or a knife or a gun or a—or any kind of harm to me, you know, and I think that's it. I don't know. I've been hurt before, and I don't know.

Bevers: I will not hurt you, nor will I allow anyone to hurt you. You are my woman. No one will bother you. No one.

La Vonne: You won't allow anyone to hurt me?

Bevers: Never. This thing you must understand. Do you understand it?

La Vonne: Yes.

Bevers: Then we should never have no problem, you and I. Go to sleep.

La Vonne: ...(inaudible) ...

Bevers: Pardon?

La Vonne: I was going to ask you...don't you have other women?

Bevers: There is a difference between women. There are women I rape. There are women I fuck, and there are you. Understand? Goodnight, Nancy. Think about what I have said.

La Vonne: I'll try. Sometimes I don't fully, you know ...

Bevers: Just do as I say and you will not be harmed. Would you like to watch me fuck your daughter? Would you? I mean, hard fuck your daughter.

La Vonne: But, you said ...

Bevers: Not be gentle...I mean hard fuck her. Would you like to watch that?

La Vonne: You said that you would not harm her.

Bevers: Would you like to watch that? Would you? That is the reason I am saying, as long as you cooperate, I will not harm you. I will not harm her. Do as I say—always!

Phone disconnects...

I AM VISIBLY SHAKEN as I hang up the phone. The last words he uttered into my ear will haunt me for years…"Do as I say—always!" If he had his way, Bevers would control me the rest of my life.

Chapter 17

Wrong Place—
Right Guy

At 12:29 A.M., Detective Martin is notified by police radio that I have received an obscene, threatening phone call, which has been traced to Bevers's workplace.

At approximately 12:30 A.M., Texas Ranger Jack Morton advises Detective Martin that Bevers was observed using the company's phone inside the building. It is confirmed via police radio that at the exact time my call was terminated, Bevers terminated his conversation. Across town, the surveillance team is elated.

"That's it! We got him!" radioed a jubilant Officer Gibbs.

An arrest warrant is immediately issued for Lanny Gene Bevers, Jr., for Retaliation. That is the only charge they can make stick right now, but it is a hell of a lot better than nothing at all.

Bevers is placed under arrest for Retaliation on January 29, 1985, Cause No. 0249373D, and Assistant District Attorney Randy Means is assigned the case. Mr. Means, like most of the young prosecutors, likes to win.

Everyone knows Bevers raped me, but the tainted identification and the mishandling of physical evidence has doomed a rape trial—for now. At least the monster will be behind bars and I will be out of danger. It is a start.

Mr. Means calls Barbara and requests that she transcribe the tapes. She dutifully sequesters herself in her office with a dictating machine. She tells her receptionist to hold all of her calls. To get every word correct, she knows, will take her complete concentration. She realizes the tape transcripts will be used in the trial as an aid for the jurors and wants them correct and impartial. She wants to get this creep the right way.

Several times she can't hear 100 percent of what is on the tapes and types "inaudible." She has never heard the tapes, and nothing prepares her for what she hears. The content is obscene, but more disturbing to her is the sound of Bevers's voice. It literally drips with evil, hatred, and rage. His threats give her goose bumps.

After transcribing all day, she goes home where Bevers's evil voice invades her sleep. Nevertheless, day in and day out she carefully goes over every word said until she is certain she has heard and typed every word correctly.

As Barbara transcribes the tapes, she catches Bevers's reference to a "Heller." He had said, "I'm sorry I had to leave town for a while. But, since they found that bitch, Heller, I had to leave town." I had never understood what he said that night.

Barbara stops and replays the section several times before she is sure of what he said.

In Fort Worth, during 1984 and 1985, twelve young, attractive, intelligent, single women were murdered. One of the serial killer's victims, Cynthia Heller, a beautiful Texas Christian University (TCU) student, had been found murdered near the campus.

Barbara remembers Ms. Heller, because in the newspaper picture she looked so stunningly beautiful, so full of hope for the future. A young woman with such promise, killed—just because someone else wanted it that way. She could not help but notice the comparison between Ms. Heller and her own daughter.

After she quits shaking, she contacts the prosecutor and tells him she has something he has to listen to—immediately. She takes the tape over to Mr. Means's office and listens to Bevers bringing Heller's death into the conversation. This makes Bevers an immediate suspect in the serial killings. Mr. Means picks up the phone and calls the task force working on the murders. He informs them they should listen to this portion of the tape.

The task force team investigates Bevers. Subsequently, they question Bevers about the murders. Bevers is not charged in connection with these crimes. I begin to wonder if he was just trying to scare me by this statement about Ms. Heller or if he really did have something to do with the murder. No one will ever know, but it is strange that he disappeared shortly after Cynthia Heller's body was found, and then returned to town and made reference to it in his call to me.

When Barbara finishes transcribing, she turns the tapes and the transcript over to the prosecutor, Mr. Means. When Mr. Means finishes listening to the tapes, he calls Barbara back into his office.

"Barbara," he says, "you know this lady better than anyone. I have just one question I'd like to ask you." Barbara nods and waits for the question. "Why hasn't she blown her fucking brains out?" The question does not surprise Barbara, given the content of the tapes.

She looks at him and simply replies, "You'd just have to know her, Randy. She's got a faith that few people ever know. She calls upon that faith to give her the strength to pull through this. I admire her more than anyone I've ever known."

He shrugs, as if he still doesn't understand the kind of strength Barbara is talking about.

Before Bevers is ever brought to trial for the retaliation calls, the file is reassigned several times. Eventually it winds up on David Montague's desk.

After months of torturing me, Bevers is caged like the animal he is—caught by his own phone calls. I can go to bed at night assured he will not kick my door in and kill me. It is an uphill battle just to get the Retaliation case to trial; the possibility of ever trying Bevers for rape is looking more and more dismal.

Additional charges are prepared to prosecute Bevers for a parole violation stemming from the 1977 rape conviction. The gloves are off—the fight for justice is about to begin. More importantly, my nightmare is almost over, whereas Bevers's has just begun.

Chapter 18

Trouble
on the Job

When I return to work on October 17, everyone is nice and kind, trying to help me around. At break time they get me a Coke, because I have trouble maneuvering the stairs. At first, it is subtle; I don't notice the change. I hear people talking behind my back. The offers to help come less and less. It even seems that I am actually chided for not doing my share of work, even when I am still disabled and on crutches.

It seems as though the women are afraid. If this can happen to me, it can happen to one of them. They seem to want to distance themselves from me more each day.

I can see the stares and hear the whispers going on around me. Going to work each day becomes a task. I am physically hurt and emotionally abandoned by those I need the most support from: my coworkers. I don't understand. Are they afraid the attacker will seek me out at work, putting them at risk? Or have I done something to dramatically change things? I try to buckle down and work harder, but it doesn't seem to be enough to satisfy anybody these days.

These are the same people who doted on me at the hospital, bringing me flowers and gifts, telling me everything was going to be all right. Suddenly, they seem to be my enemies. I am hurt and don't understand why this is happening.

I call Barbara. It surprises me to learn that the prosecutors do not want women on a panel in a jury trial involving rape. If a female juror feels the victim has done nothing to place herself in jeopardy, then that juror also could be vulnerable to rape. She tells me she suspects that many of the women at work feel that I am a reminder of what can happen to a person in the sanctity of her own home. No one wants to feel that vulnerable, so they try to place some degree of guilt on the victim. Barbara encourages me to ignore these people and try to do my job to the best of my ability.

I tell Barbara that there is an uncomfortable feeling in the air. I say it is like one of the days before I went back to work and my coworkers visited my home. I struggled with the piano to play them a song. It was not long before they got antsy and wanted to leave.

Feeling all these changes and possible repercussions on my job, I ask Barbara to call Jane Bingham at Rape Crisis for me. She says she will.

Jane Bingham comes to the school and visits with Mr. Dodd and the assistant director of personnel to talk to them about how victims feel and act after an attack. She lets them know, basically, what to expect from me—especially given the physical injuries I have suffered. They just want Jane to "fix" me back the way I was before the rape, as if I were a broken doll.

I know my job is in jeopardy, so I make a list of changes or improvements that can be implemented to help the situation, but none are implemented. I feel the kiss of death coming. Shortly thereafter, the personnel director tells me there will be a panel meeting in January 1985. Sure enough, I am placed on probation for a two- to three-month period. Physical injuries aside, I feel I have been doing my job the same as before. Why do I have to keep being hurt?

It becomes clear to me that I better start looking for a new job, before I am fired or asked to resign. Helen Corbitt, a friend of my friend, Carol, has built a business into a printing company in Dallas. Helen is willing to let me interview.

The personnel director calls me in and tells me things are not working out here, and I am going to be assigned to another school. My new title is: Teacher's Aide. I am angry, but what can I do? This is not my field of work, and I really feel out of place. But, to hold on to my poverty-level wages of nine thousand dollars a year, I will try to make the best of it. I had gone from a fourteen-thousand-dollar annual salary in 1982 to this new low of a nine-thousand-dollar annual salary in 1985. I am deeply depressed. It seems Bevers is now taking food out of my mouth, too.

At the new school, things do not seem to be any better. It is just a matter of time before the school principal calls me in and tells me I do not seem to be working out. Like a little school girl being sent to the principal's office, I am sent back to the personnel director for a new assignment. I feel embarrassed and humiliated, like a failure, having to go back to the director in front of my old coworkers who once had been my dear friends.

They decide I should go to a school for mentally ill and disturbed children. Already, there has been a lot of discussion about this school closing because of lack of funding.

I drive into the parking lot of my new place of employment. My hands are clammy and I am literally shaking when I pull up. It is to be my first and last day on the job. I go in and meet my supervisor. I am shown around and then instructed to take inventory in one of the school's storage rooms, which is full of toys. I have a legal pad and am busy with the inventory until lunch, when I venture to look around. This place looks more like a prison than a school. There are big metal locks on the doors and steel mesh on the windows.

I hurry into a kitchen area with a steel door. I call my mother to discuss the situation. She tells me to hang in there, when an eleven-year-old girl bursts in and grabs the hair on the back of my head and starts pulling it out. As I try to get the girl off of me and explain the ordeal on the phone to my mother, the scene is total chaos. There are three other people attempting to get the child off me, too. But the girl is extremely strong and keeps pulling at my hair, yanking back my head and reinjuring the neck muscles that were injured in the assault.

As soon as the girl is pulled off me, I tell the school officials that I have reinjured myself and clock out to go to my mother's house. I file for worker's compensation, because of the injury. I have been placed in the worst situation that anyone who has been emotionally and physically abused can be. It is like they want me to quit.

After a short time on worker's compensation, I decide I have had enough and give my two-week notice. It is near the end of 1985. I am already starting to train for my new job at the printing company, though I find it difficult to concentrate.

I notice I am gaining weight and this bothers me a lot. Prior to the attack, I had a very nice, slim figure. My only comfort these days seems to be in food.

I manage to hold on to this job until June 1986, when the economy forces layoffs. The company reduces its work force by 50 percent. I have only worked there for seven months, and, of course, the last to come in is the first to go. They lay me off.

Actually, I am a little relieved, but scared. I need time to work on my testimony and get the petitions signed to keep Bevers in jail as long as possible. At the same time, I need a job to pay the bills, and want to find something in the clerical area.

I find a job as a "floater" in a church, helping the other clerical staff for minimum wage. They say I can stay here as long as I like. I am there only a short while when I find a job with an airline company. I jump at the chance because it pays so much better and I will have some benefits, which I need for my daughter as well as myself.

I know even if Bevers is sent to prison, he will get out again. I hope I will be able to stay here until I can get a new identity, and with it, a new job, so Bevers can never find me.

Chapter 19

Where Is Justice?

No one in the DA's office wants to have anything to do with this case. It is difficult to listen to the tapes. Besides, if the state gets a conviction, retaliation is all they could go after, since the rape case has been so badly botched. Barbara says that retaliation is a non-violent crime and carries little time in prison. Time is what I need and need badly. I have to get out of that house, change my identity, and do it all before Bevers can get out and get to me.

Assistant District Attorney David Montague is young, handsome, and has a reputation for winning. Barbara says from the way he talks to the way he is so sure of himself, he reminds her of the Kennedy brothers. This is the kind of attorney she feels I need. So, when Barbara finds out that he is the prosecutor in the Retaliation case, she begins to rest a little better.

Mr. Montague is given all the tapes and the transcripts. Later in the week, he summons Barbara to his office. He asks her to set up an appointment with Michelle, Barbara, and me, to meet him on Sunday. Barbara calls and tells me how wonderful he is.

On Sunday, she greets us at the elevator. On our ride in the elevator to the third floor to meet Mr. Montague, Barbara can tell I am nervous. We know each other well, and she tries to soothe my doubts by again telling me he is one of the best prosecutors in town.

We step out of the elevator, and Barbara walks to him. "Oh no, he's sick!" she says. He does look ill. He tells her he doesn't feel good because he thinks is coming down with the flu. Great! She needs that "on-his-toes, on-top-of-everything-attorney," and instead she is looking at a prosecutor who might throw up any minute.

With much trepidation, she brings Michelle and me in and introduces us to Mr. Montague. Instantly, Michelle likes him and he likes her. I am still cautious. Michelle and I sit directly in front of his desk, while Barbara sits off to the side.

Michelle and Mr. Montague are able to joke around, but with me, the conversation is strained. I seem to get negative vibrations from this man, even though it is obvious he has put some time in on this case. The files of my ordeal are strung across his desk, together with all those horrible tapes.

I immediately voice my concerns to Mr. Montague. If we can't get Bevers on the rape case, which is looking more and more doubtful, then I want to get as much time as possible on the retaliation charge.

Things seem cordial as Mr. Montague asks questions of both Michelle and me, with Barbara interjecting information now and again. From the beginning of the meeting, Barbara and I are both clear that this is a pre-trial sit-down to prepare to go to trial on the retaliation case.

The conversation continues, and I can see by the look of consternation on Barbara's face that she senses an annoyance developing between Mr. Montague and me.

I tell him, "Get him and put him away as long as you can." He responds, "Putting him away on this case might not be worth the trouble of a trial." Given the light sentence for such a charge, the "good time" Bevers has accumulated waiting for the trial might just result in his being able to walk out of the court-room, even if he is found guilty. Things are not looking very good, to say the least.

Then Mr. Montague tells me, "Look, La Vonne, I don't see any chance of ever getting this guy on the rape case. It was just too botched up by the police and your misidentification. Our best shot is getting him for Retaliation. Personally, I think we should let him plead guilty. His lawyer says he'll plead guilty in exchange for a twelve-year term. If we take him to trial on the retaliation charge and win, the most we can get is twenty years. Frankly, with 'good time,' it's not going to make that much difference, even if we get the maximum sentence. Michelle and you will have to go through a lot for nothing. And, as far as the rape trial goes, well, I think we've just lost any chance of trying that!"

Barbara holds her breath knowing all hell is about to break loose. She knows my frustration...my state of mind. She is frustrated, too. Mr. Montague is telling me that Bevers is going to get away with the vicious rape after all, and I am sick of it. I glance over at Barbara. My anger has been simmering under the surface. Now it is starting to boil. I have literally gone through hell with the attacker as well as the judicial system. I'm still fragile, and Mr. Montague is taking too rough of an edge with such a delicate subject.

My anger begins to boil over. "I don't care. Twelve years is not enough! I want to go to trial!"

Mr. Montague's reply is curt. "Well, my inclination is to not try this thing at all—just let him plead!"

I angrily retort, "You just let him go! I'll handle it! I'll take this matter into my own hands!"

Mr. Montague, just as angry, warns, "You do, and I'll have to prosecute you!"

My voice raises almost to a scream. "So prosecute me!"

That is it. The explosion. Through all of the perils, horrors, taunts, traps, and pain, I have remained even-tempered. Now, I fly into a violent rage. I jump up from my chair, walk around Mr. Montague's desk, and approach him, screaming, "You try to live with this!" as I shove my mutilated hand in the young prosecutor's face. "He raped me, sodomized me, severed my thumb, broke my leg, and terrorized me with phone calls for months, and you want to just let him plead guilty and get twelve years!" I continue to scream, incredulous at even the thought of this possibility. "Twelve years is nothing! He's already served enough time in jail to get out as soon as he's sentenced. I need help! I need protection!" I proclaim, still violently thrusting my thumbless hand under Mr. Montague's nose. "You try living in this nightmare he's created in my life!"

Mr. Montague's face turns beet red. Just as quickly as it started, it is over. Quiet fills the room.

Barbara jumps to her feet and implores, "La Vonne, let's go in the other room and try to calm down." She turns, holding me in her arms, to face Mr. Montague, his red face now turning back to its pasty white, and says, "David, let's take a break. Give us some time. This is really hard on her."

Mr. Montague nods, and Barbara and I leave his office and head for one of the investigator's offices, leaving my bubbly daughter behind to visit with Mr. Montague, a man I now despise. Barbara closes the door behind us and says, "Look, La Vonne, I don't blame you for being angry. Mr. Montague just isn't feeling well, and I really don't think he meant to come across as unconcerned. He really does want to get this guy. Let's try to work together, or this whole thing will fall apart." Barbara knows he's the only one willing to take this on and fears now he's going to drop it!

During a twenty-minute break, Barbara attempts to calm me down. She gets me something to drink, makes me promise to try and be more calm, and above all, tells me not to leave. I reluctantly agree to her terms, and she sighs with relief. Poor Barbara, no wonder she has ulcers! She knows if I leave that will be it. Bevers will plead guilty and then he will walk out a free man—and I will probably be dead before long. We still have no rape case to build an indictment on, and Barbara and I have no doubt that his first trip will be to my house to finish the job.

While we are taking our break, Michelle and Mr. Montague are talking and developing a great rapport. They just hit it off. Barbara feels Michelle might be our saving grace, because, if I am in danger, so is Michelle, and Mr. Montague likes this young girl. We head back to Mr. Montague's office.

Mr. Montague is calmer and starts out quietly. "La Vonne, look, I'm frustrated, because I should be able to protect you and Michelle from this guy, but I can't! That's what's so frustrating—I can't protect you. Look, let's go over the facts again. If you want a trial, you're going to get one, okay?"

We are ecstatic. I take a deep breath and say, "Okay, Mr. Montague, what do you want to know?"

The trial is on again. Mr. Montague admits for the first time he has not listened to the tapes but will go through them the next week. Barbara can see the look of anger on my face, and I probably surprise her when I manage to keep my cool. The next few hours are spent with Mr. Montague painstakingly going over the unfamiliar contents of the tapes with Michelle and me in preparation for the trial.

Despite the outburst, the meeting ends on a positive note. I believe Mr. Montague is sincere in his desire to help us.

The next week will be spent with more meetings, going over my log and the tapes. We will list on a note pad those things said on the tapes that are indicative that Bevers is the rapist. A lot of hard work is ahead of us all.

Chapter 20

History Repeats Itself

Everyone knows that Bevers raped me in the fall of 1984; a revenge attack, just like he had warned me. But now the identification of the rapist is tainted. We all also know a defense attorney can make mincemeat out of my identification.

At the moment Bevers is in jail on the retaliation charge, but I know I will have to get him on the rape charge to put him away long enough for me to build a new life—and a new identity. I don't doubt that he'll return when he is freed. Bevers is one of the small percentage of criminals who come back to get their victims.

Michelle and I start carefully reconstructing both rapes; the similarities we find are eerie. Both the 1977 and 1984 attacks were alike in that both entries were made by the attacker through the garage, then through the kitchen door to gain access into the house. The same physical description fit the attacker. Both times the attacker had spoken in a soft, whispering voice when he wasn't screaming orders.

In the 1977 rape, a thirteen-inch butcher knife was held under my chin; in the 1984 rape, the attacker held a .44 magnum gun under my chin and had a knife behind his back in the waistband of his jeans. Both times I was instructed not to look at my attacker. The attacker posed me in front of the bathroom mirror, and his head would jerk spasmodically as he held me there.

During both of the attacks, the attacker would look at my reflection and then, with his head shaking, he would look directly at me. The attacker in both rapes used the term "lady" when talking to me.

In both attacks, the attacker seemed to be manic, slipping in and out of Jekyll and Hyde personas, being mean one minute and becoming apologetic for hurting me the next. The attacker in both incidents hated the sight of blood. He used towels to wash the blood up when he slashed my finger in the 1977 attack, and did the same when he horribly mutilated me in 1984.

In the 1984 attack, when the sight of blood bothered the attacker, he went straight to the linen closet as if he knew it was there, and gathered towels to soak up my spilled blood. He also called me "Nancy," the name he had heard me referred to during the 1977 trial. I always go by my middle name, La Vonne.

In both the 1977 and 1984 rapes, my attacker posed the same question to me, using the exact same words: "How long has it been since you have been fucked?" The attacker inserted two fingers in my vagina in both rapes. His penis was mostly flaccid in both attacks, only getting hard as his anger grew. The attacker did not ejaculate in either attack. Both times, he wiped the blood off the floor using a circular motion as he worked. And the attacker smoked Marlboro cigarettes in my presence during both attacks.

In the 1977 attack I suffered a large laceration to the right index finger and a bruise on the kidney from the doorknob jabbed into my back. During the 1984 attack my injuries were complete amputation of the right thumb, plus multiple blunt and sharp injuries, with a fracture to my right tibia and fibula, and pulled neck and back muscles from being dragged by my hair, and wounds sustained to the head from the blows of the butt of the gun.

It seemed the similarities were endless. This was the same guy—no doubt about it. Unfortunately, he had learned his lesson in the first attack, having been convicted from a fingerprint found when he picked up the glass he had broken. He had smartened up and used gloves the second time so as not to leave any prints. It looked like it had worked. Bevers had not wasted his six years in prison. He had gotten a good "education" from other inmates.

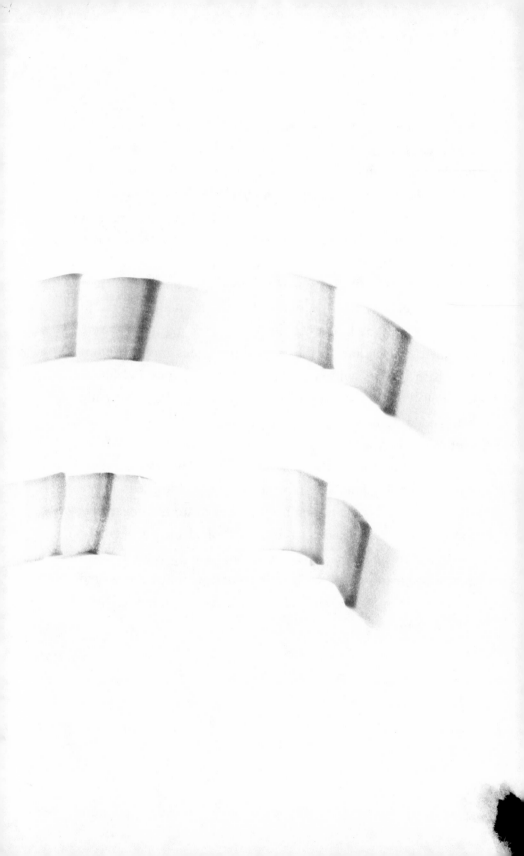

Chapter 21

The Retaliation Trial

The retaliation trial of Lanny Gene Bevers, Jr. begins in July 1987, in the Honorable Judge Joe Drago's Criminal District Court No. 4. Bevers's family is all here in support of him, sitting behind him on the defense side. His lawyer, Mike Thomas, busily works on some papers.

On the prosecutor's side are the two prosecutors, Mr. Montague and Mike Parrish (more seasoned as a prosecutor than Mr. Montague). Mr. Parrish was also Barbara's boss before she became a coordinator. She has told me how much she respects and likes Mike Parrish. I don't know him, but according to Barbara, he is a good, kind, intelligent man. I am lucky to have this team! Behind them sit Barbara, Michelle, friends of ours, and me.

One of my staunchest supporters is a lady named Fern Gant. In true Texas tradition, Fern is "tough as leather and made out of baling wire" as we Texans are proud of describing ourselves. Fern is a strong tower for me to lean on, and I am especially glad she is here.

Another friend I rely on is Carol Nanchy. She is the dear friend who watched over me during my hospital stay and gave me the cute little doll dubbed "the victim doll" that eventually winds up in Barbara's possession. She uses the doll as a reminder not to forget the victims, because it seems criminals have all the rights.

We feel good about the trial because our evidence is solid and the prosecutors are the best. I can't help but worry, though, because this trial will be the first time I will see Bevers in person since the attack.

Michelle is so frightened of Bevers she temporarily dyes her beautiful brown hair blond to disguise herself in the event he tries to find her after the trial. After the second attack, until I found it, Michelle had slept with a thirteen-inch butcher knife between her mattresses. She said she would not be without a weapon.

We all hold our breath as they bring out Bevers. He does not look like the monster Barbara has pictured. He looks like he wouldn't hurt a fly. He has the jail-house pallor, a yellow tint to his skin, and has lost a lot of weight. He does not seem so horrifying in his jail-house greens. It is also obvious that he doesn't have a jury to impress (he had chosen a trial before the court called a "bench trial"), so he wears the jail clothes as opposed to the military outfit he wore in his first trial. His jail-house uniform will suffice; he knows the Judge is already aware he is serving time.

All that worry I had about my embarrassing conversations with Bevers is now behind me. A judge will understand what was going on without question.

Barbara and I both think Bevers's family is strange. His wife, attractive and supportive, is someone I feel he doesn't deserve on his side. His mother also is an attractive woman, on the outside, but that's where it stops. Throughout the trial she shows a vindictive, hateful side, almost taunting me as she goes in and out of the courtroom. Carol Bevers Baker Hall goes out of her way to make eye contact with both Michelle and me. She goes to extremes, making a spectacle of herself by sneering and laughing out loud at inappropriate times in the courtroom. Her outbreaks cause Judge Drago to cast several stern looks in her direction.

It is obvious from the start, as my liaison, that Barbara has her work cut out for her. She is the conduit to keep Bevers's family from harassing and rattling Michelle and me throughout the trial. Mrs. Hall is not going to make that an easy task for Barbara. But, I am not worried. I know that Barbara, although tiny, is feisty. She isn't about to be intimated by anyone. As if she doesn't have enough to occupy her, she also has her hands full trying to intervene between my daughter and me. Tensions are high, and we argue constantly. Of course, most teenagers Michelle's age argue with their mothers, but in this case there is ample reason for more than the normal tension involved in mother/daughter quarreling. We are both nervous and scared.

As the trial begins, Michelle and I are not put in the witness room, but allowed to stay in court, since the defense did not ask for "the rule" to be invoked. The tapes are introduced into evidence, and the long, arduous task of listening to them and following the transcript begins.

Witnesses come and go. The security man for Bell Telephone testifies to the tap and the record of the calls traced back to Bevers's place of employment and his father-in-law's house. A voice analysis expert, who had worked with Bevers while attending college, testifies that the voice on the tape is Bevers. He also mentions that "Lanny" was always trying to perfect a Spanish accent at work, but that he didn't do it very well. The Texas Rangers testify about the stakeout and the eventual arrest of Bevers.

Then Michelle is put on the stand and asked about each call on the tapes she had personally taken. For a fifteen-year-old, she has had to grow up too fast. She has been subjected to language no young girl should have to listen to, and she is highly nervous as she sits so close to the man responsible for the terror that has gone on so long in her life. She is frightened, too, that he will pay her back, the way he had paid me back for testifying against him in the first rape trial. She has plenty of reasons to be nervous and afraid.

Strong and gutsy, my little girl sits straight up and, with a determined look in her eyes, smiles at Barbara, who sits on the front row so they can establish good eye contact, and prepares herself for an onslaught of questions from both sides. After establishing some basic information about name and address, Mr. Montague plunges ahead.

Mr. Montague: "When did you get the first unusual phone call, about?"

"Somewhere around the 22nd of October."

"What year?"

"1984."

"Do you remember much about that phone call?"

"I just remember a man's voice asking me if...well, I answered the phone, and he said, 'Is this Michelle?' and I said, 'Yes,' and I go, 'Who is this?' and he goes, 'Michelle,' and then he started, you know, saying ugly things."

"What were the ugly things that he said?"

"That he was going to...ummm..."

"It's all right to use the words that he said."

"That he was the man that fucked my mom, and then he started into this heavy breathing, and I just hung up after that."

"What did you do at that time?"

"I told my mom that it was a bad phone call, and I started crying and everything, and I told her that it sounded like the man that was in our house."

The Judge, sensing Michelle's discomfort, calls for a short break, and then the trial resumes.

Mr. Montague: "Between that call on the eighth and the call on the fifteenth, to your knowledge, had your mother gotten any of these kind of phone calls?"

"Yes. Like country and western music calls and stuff like that. Nobody speaking, though."

It flashes through Barbara's mind that I had mentioned calls back before the first rape occurred where just country and western music had played in the background, with no conversation. Another link in the chain.

"Let me hand you what has been marked as State's Exhibit 1, and I want you to open that and pull whatever's inside out."

Michelle complies.

"Now, what has been marked as State's Exhibit 1A, is that what you pulled out of that envelope, State's Exhibit 1?"

"Yes, sir, it is."

"What is State's Exhibit No. 1A?"

"The tape."

"It is the cassette tape?"

"Yes."

"Now, I want you to listen to this, Michelle. Let me ask you this: Back on December 15th, when you got that call and you recorded that tape—"

"Uh huh—"

"—did you listen to that tape?"

"Yes, I did."

"How long after you got the call did you listen to that tape?"

"About five minutes after."

"Have you heard that same conversation since then, that same tape?"

"Yes, sir."

"How many times?"

"About three."

"Michelle?"

"Uh, huh."

"Now, I want you to listen to part of the tape which has been marked as State's Exhibit 1A, okay?"

"Okay."

State's Exhibit 1A is played.

The Court: "Let the record reflect that the witness, Michelle Skalias, has listened to the tape with earphones and the defendant and defendant's attorney and the prosecutors all have sets of earphones and listened to the tape, and the Court did, too."

Michelle is asked if the recording is a fair and accurate recording and if it has been altered in any way. Michelle responds that it has not been altered and is a true and accurate recording. And so it goes, as each tape is marked and played.

Michelle is brave and concise. A prosecutor couldn't have asked for a better witness. Michelle flashes a smile at Barbara (she is still mad at me), and Barbara flashes one back. We both know she has done a great job, and she has made it through without falling apart. Some tough kid! Barbara makes it clear how much she admires Michelle and all she had been through. She is doing what she had to do. Michelle had to grow up fast. Barbara says she can't help but reflect back to her own fifteen-year-old, Lisa, and thank God she has been spared all that Michelle has lived through in her young life.

Then I have my turn. Barbara tells me she knows I will be every bit as courageous and accurate as my daughter. Barbara can't help but wince when I am sworn in and raise that mutilated right hand. Barbara thinks I am courageous; she has told me on more than one occasion how much she admires me.

After hearing all the evidence, Judge Drago finds Lanny Gene Bevers, Jr., guilty of Retaliation and sentences him to fifteen years in prison. Barbara is upset. Fifteen years is only three more years than the earlier discussed plea bargain, and five years less than the maximum for this crime. How could this judge listen to those awful tapes and not sentence Bevers to the maximum of twenty years?

She calms down, and seeks Judge Drago out in his chambers, asking if she may speak with him. He agrees, and she expresses her feelings. He explains he has backed off from the possible twenty-year sentence, hoping Bevers will not appeal his ruling.

She is somewhat appeased, but still angry Bevers did not get the maximum. In the end, he does appeal the ruling. The irony of it all is that he had enough "good time" served to get out. It is his appeal keeping him in prison. In Texas, if you get a sentence of fifteen years or more, you are not allowed to make bond and get out while your case is on appeal. Which means Bevers is still in jail, for now.

Chapter 22

No Relief in Sight

This trial brought no good news, just as David Montague had said. But at least Bevers knew we were serious about forging ahead. He did not know, although I'm sure he suspected, that we didn't have much to go on with the rape case. If we had, he would have been indicted.

So Bevers goes back to jail, and Barbara and I wonder what to do from this point. She tells me to immediately start gathering signatures for a petition to the parole board, asking that Bevers be held in jail for as long as possible. Barbara has a difficult time selling me on the worthiness of this project, but it becomes one of the most positive things I do on my own to keep Bevers in jail.

In the aftermath of the Retaliation verdict, we all have to keep searching for a way to get Bevers on trial for brutally raping me. We have a long way to go and many people to talk to before that day.

Chapter 23

Trouble at Home

Michelle has become withdrawn and moody from all that has transpired. I am very worried about her. She has isolated herself and is very depressed. She will not express her feelings. She has always tried to protect me, and now she is angry at herself and at me. Often, the first time I am aware of how she feels is when I hear her door slam or she is literally crying on the phone to her grandparents or friends. She has always been a leader and felt challenged by learning new things, especially concerning sports. Since the attack she has refused to try anything new. Sometimes, I have to coax her into getting dressed for school, church, or other activities. I am beginning to fear that the attacker has taken away her childhood.

During one of the school's parent-teacher meetings, I talk with Michelle's physical education teacher, whom Michelle holds in high regard. I really like the teacher and feel she has a positive influence on Michelle. She is aware of what happened and is concerned about Michelle. She begins working with her. First, she makes her scorekeeper and gives her a whistle—a pretty great thing for a seventh grader. Second, she tells her she doesn't have to dress out for class, she can wear her jeans.

One day the coach takes Michelle into a closet, away from everyone. She says, "I'm going to tell you right now, if you don't get your head together you are going to go down the tubes with this thing. I would hate to see someone who has leadership quality, and has the potential to do better, fail. If you get your head together, I know you can move forward and not let this incident pull you down."

It is a turning point for Michelle. She respects the coach, and her lecture makes Michelle stop and think. It does more for her than anything or anyone else.

The coach encourages Michelle to try out for the cheerleading squad, which Michelle does, and she makes the team. I had no idea Michelle was so popular. I am so pleased Michelle has proved herself and accomplished what we already knew she could do! Everyone in the school seems supportive of Michelle, too.

Once out of her shell, she returns to being a gregarious budding teenager with lots of friends.

Now, there are other problems. It seems the stress will never let up. Adolescence is hard enough without people like Lanny Bevers jumping in to stir up the pot, so to speak.

Michelle and I are not getting along, to put it mildly. Barbara's phone will ring, and Barbara will pick it up to hear either Michelle or me on the other end having had it "up to here" with one another.

I feel Michelle is angry at me, hates me; however, Michelle is just angry and scared. She wants out of the house and away from her mother, both reminders of all the really horrible moments in her life.

When Michelle and I reach a standoff, one of us will wind up calling Barbara to intervene. She talks to both of us and helps us work out solutions to the many problems that exist.

We have the normal "on-the-phone-too-long," "not-doing-your-homework," arguments that all mothers and daughters experience. But the arguments have become more intense since the second rape and the terrorizing phone calls. We begin to take all our frustrations out on each other.

Michelle begins to act out. She becomes violent. When we have arguments, it might be days before she will come out of her room, and then only for food, water, or the bathroom.

When Michelle is upset with her boyfriend, she kicks holes in the wall, curses at him and at me, and stomps back to her room, slamming the door. It gets so bad that we both decide to seek counseling to learn how to handle our anger. But even this doesn't help. Our lives are in turmoil, a living hell.

Today it turns into unbridled rage. Michelle and Tracey, the cheerleading squad's captain, are practicing their cheers over at our house. I have gotten on Michelle many times about not doing the dishes and cleaning up after herself. The phone rings as I listen to the girls practice their cheers. It is Larry, my ex-fiancé. I stand in the kitchen listening to his guilt-ridden excuses as to why our relationship broke up. It is bad enough dealing with Bevers's phone calls over the past months, but I have to endure Larry's intrusions over the phone even longer. After the uncomfortable conversation is over, I angrily slam down the phone. I've had it with both jerks. I do not even want to answer the phone anymore.

I glance in the cabinet and see the set of dishes I bought for our much-talked-about wedding. Unable to control my anger over the total disruption in my life, I begin to smash dish after dish on the linoleum floor.

Michelle comes running in, angrily accusing me of causing a scene and embarrassing her in front of company because of a few dishes that have not been washed. She has no inkling about the phone call. Michelle reaches for a dish and angrily smashes it to the floor. Here we are, mother and daughter, smashing dish after dish until there are none left to smash.

Afterwards, Michelle can tell by the look on my face that the dish smashing has nothing to do with her lackadaisical attitude toward helping with the housework. She tries to soothe me, saying, "Mom, you need to sit down and rest! I'll clean up this mess. Please sit down!

"Tracey, I'm sorry this happened while you were here. It's over now. Let's make the best of the rest of the evening. I really do want you to stay over tonight and practice our yells."

I sit on the couch and watch my daughter clean up the mess we have made in our fit of rage. I vow I will never let a man get this close to me again. My heart has been broken too many times.

Other flare-ups between Michelle and me prompt her to hurl kitchen chairs, made of heavy iron, in my direction. Sometimes she throws the telephone across the room, with me as the target. We actually get into a fistfight with each other, pulling hair and punching each other; there is just so much anger to get out. During these really hard times, we try to just stay out of each other's way.

Michelle internalizes her anger; she does not want to talk to anyone about the Bevers case. The only people she will open up to about Bevers are Barbara and Mr. Montague.

Barbara keeps harping on me to buy a gun and learn how to use it. She says she will even teach me how to use it and clean it. Little does she know that a gun at this point could be used against me by Michelle or vice versa. Things are just out of control in our lives.

The arguments between us get so bad that Michelle moves out for about a year and lives with a friend, Robin Heston. Although it ultimately turns out for the best, I feel abandoned and so alone. I sink deeper and deeper into depression.

Michelle is now staying with another friend, Christy. I really feel uneasy about this move, though I can't say why. Come to find out, Christy's older sister, Patty, is friends with Lanny Bevers's sister, Deena. One day Michelle happens to glance at a photograph on Christy's dresser; it is a picture of Patty posing with Mike—Lanny Bevers's brother. Michelle grabs everything she can hold that belongs to her and flees out the back door.

Later, Christy tells Michelle what a good guy Bevers is, and how she and I just must be mistaken. It is a process almost like trying to "brainwash" Michelle so she will not cooperate and testify at the trial.

Michelle moves back home. It seems time matures her; we are finally out of each other's hair. We start to become friends again and join forces to see Lanny Bevers put away for as long as possible!

Chapter 24

Battle for Justice

I call Barbara and say, "We have got to get a game plan, Barbara. No one else seems to care. What are we going to do?"

Barbara starts making a list. She tells me to call Rape Crisis and get Jane Bingham and Linda Braswell to stir up some dust by calling Tim Curry's key assistant, Anita McKesson. The idea is to push on this case until we start getting some feedback. Right now the case just lays there, waiting for the statute of limitations to run out on it. If that happens, nothing can be done even if Bevers announces on the courthouse steps that he's my tormentor.

Barbara tells me to call Victims of Violence and see if they can start harping at Anita, too. She also volunteers to pay Anita a visit on my case, which she does. When she goes in, Anita has all my files and asks Barbara to have a seat and tell her a little more about the case. She fills Anita in on what is going on, and tells Anita she feels my life and my daughter's are in jeopardy if we do not get this case to trial. Anita promises to talk to Mr. Curry, the DA, and see what can be done.

Barbara calls me and tells me the National Victim Center is moving its headquarters to Fort Worth. I call there and tell my story to Linda Barker-Lowrance. She does a lot of networking and gets the word out; pressure is placed on Mr. Curry to do something with the case.

Barbara then advises me to sit down and write a heartfelt letter to Mr. Curry explaining my dilemma and asking him to act on my behalf.

Mr. Curry empathizes with me and then does what should have been done a long time ago: He puts Mr. Montague on the case because he is familiar with it, and then he puts an unassuming prosecutor by the name of Alan Levy in charge of the case.

Chapter 25

David and Goliath

David is Mr. Montague. Goliath, as Barbara and I call him, is Alan Levy. He seems laid-back and looks like nothing could ever rattle him. He is the Chief of the Criminal Assistant District Attorney's Section. The chief usually does not try cases. But then Mr. Levy is anything but the usual. To look at him, you might think he'd be okay in court, but to see the magic web he spins in a courtroom will make you a true believer. He isn't extremely personable and it doesn't seem to bother him. He cares about one thing: getting the job done and done right, which means a guilty verdict with the highest sentence available.

He is a very heavy smoker, constantly going around with a cigarette either in his mouth or hanging between his fingers. His "vice" will prove invaluable in getting the rape case to trial. The first time I meet with Mr. Levy, he is all business, quiet, sincere, and gentle.

Mr. Levy and Mr. Montague go over and over the files trying to find something they can hang on Bevers. When Barbara goes to visit Mr. Levy, he seems distressed. He tells her how frustrating it is because almost all of the evidence has been lost or destroyed. The identification has been tainted because I picked out two people as the offender, neither of them Bevers. She asks him why Bevers has never been presented before me in any of the lineups or photo identifications to do with the second rape. He shrugs his shoulders and shakes his head in bewilderment.

Barbara is in her office working when Mr. Levy calls her to come in to his office. When she walks in he has a huge grin on his face and says, "I think we got him. If we just haven't gone over the statute of limitations. I'm fixing to look it up right now." Barbara sits down too nervous to even breathe. Mr. Levy slams the book shut and exclaims, "All right! We're safe. We're going to go before the Grand Jury immediately."

Barbara can't stand it any longer, "What is it, Alan? What's the breakthrough?"

Mr. Levy grins smugly and puts his lit cigarette into an ashtray on his desk. "You know he was wearing gloves, right?" he toys with her.

"Right," she replies, anxious to hear the rest.

"You know we dusted the lighter that dropped out of his pocket and didn't get any prints?"

"Right," she replies once again. She knows he knows something, and she is dying to know what it is.

"Well, being a smoker, I decided that we might just be able to get a fingerprint to identify Bevers by dusting the cylinder of the lighter." Mr. Levy says.

Barbara has a confused look on her face. Mr. Levy, amused, continues, "The cylinder is what holds the lighter fluid in the lighter and makes it go."

"Oh, okay, I got it," she says, feeling a little stupid. After all, her dad's a heavy smoker and she has seen him fill those cylinders all her life.

Mr. Levy continues, "Well, the lab not only got a print off that cylinder, they got an identifiable print, and guess whose it is? One Lanny Gene Bevers, Jr.," he says. Barbara sits there in disbelief. For almost five years that lighter has sat in the evidence locker with Bevers's print right on it. After all, as Buckner said back in the late seventies, "jurors love fingerprints." And here we are with one perfectly preserved fingerprint.

Mr. Levy tells Barbara to get me on the phone and set up an appointment as soon as possible.

It is Saturday when we meet. I walk in expecting to see Mr. Levy, the suit and tie man.

Instead I see Mr. Levy setting there in a Georgetown T-shirt with a big, Cheshire cat grin spread across his face. Barbara hasn't told me about the print. She feels that pleasure belongs to Mr. Levy. Needless to say, I am elated to find out that Bevers "caught himself" again, so to speak.

I excitedly take notes as Mr. Levy dictates all the things we need to get together for a trial. We will need the FBI to testify about the print, to put together a list of similarities in the first rape and the second, and to try to link information from the terroristic phone calls to the rape. For example, Bevers asked me about playing the piano in one of the phone calls. The way the piano is placed in my home, someone would have had to have been inside to know I had one; that sort of thing is what Mr. Levy wants.

From this point forward, Mr. Levy and Mr. Montague will be my heroes, my knights in shining armor. Mr. Montague and "Goliath" go to work, and so do Barbara, Michelle, and I.

Chapter 26

Going for Broke: The Second Trial

This trial will be it for me. Literally, it is the difference between living or dying. Bevers has to be found guilty and put in prison for at least long enough for me to rebuild my life and gain a new identity. This way, when he is eventually paroled, he will be unable to find me.

Bevers fires his original attorney, Leon Haley, and the court appoints Don Gandy and Tim Moore. The trial is to take place in Impact Court No. 2, Cause No. 0335130, with the Honorable Judge Harry Hopkins presiding.

Barbara does not know Mr. Gandy very well, but she and Tim Moore worked together in the District Attorney's Office before he went into private practice. Barbara describes him as a sharp, kind, gentle man who would give Bevers a better defense than he deserves. She puts me at ease by telling me Mr. Moore is a compassionate and fine lawyer. He will put on a good defense, but she doesn't think he will be insensitive to me on the stand. Attorneys really lose points with a jury if they deal unsympathetically with a rape victim, so, they have to be nice, especially when questioning someone who has been brutalized as badly as I have been.

The trial starts in November 1989, and this time, like the first trial, Bevers chooses a jury to judge him. The prosecutors are David Montague and Alan Levy.

The jury is seated and the trial begins. This time "the rule" is invoked and both Michelle and I are kept in the witness room. Always our advocate, Barbara sits in the courtroom. Since we are witnesses, she can not relay much back to either one of us other than her opinion on how things are going.

The State presents its case. I am the star witness and I tell my story in great detail, never failing or faltering. I know I have to make the jury understand why this case has gone badly from the start. Prosecutors are fond of telling their victims, "You don't worry about making the case, that's my job. Your job is just to tell your story." Nevertheless, Barbara says most victims feel it is their job to help convince the jury of what has happened to them. I am no exception.

I testify in this second rape trial a little more comfortably than I did at my first rape trial, mainly because this is my third trial to go through with Bevers. With each trial my web of friends and supporters extends.

I look the jurors in the eye when I describe Bevers cutting off my thumb. "It was like deboning a chicken," I say. "I was struggling, trying to get away from him." I notice some of the jurors wince in horror. I go on, "I was very traumatized. I feared for my life. I felt he was going to kill me at any moment."

The clincher in this trial is "the fingerprint." We think it is great. Bevers gets caught again by his own fingerprint. Barbara jokes about this, saying, "I guess it really is true when they say smoking can be detrimental to your health. It sure proved to be to Bevers."

Mr. Montague stands before the jury and holds up a huge picture of Bevers's fingerprint and explains to the jury how it was found on the cylinder of the lighter dropped by the rapist in my bedroom. We know we have him, finally!

Bevers elects not to testify, because all of his past history can be brought before the jury—if he takes the stand and "opens the door." For example, if the prosecutor asks if he has ever been in trouble before or Bevers denies being in trouble, his past actions can be used against him. He really does not have much of a choice, anyway. Besides, what can you say when an FBI fingerprint expert says that's your fingerprint on the lighter found in the victim's house?

Watching Alan Levy in final arguments before the jury is like watching a genius at work. He is good. Real good! Don't get me wrong. David gave a great summation, too. But Alan just has a gift and rapport with the jury that is unique.

It doesn't take long for the jury to come back with a guilty verdict. Bevers decided at the beginning of the trial to have the Judge set his sentence in the event of his conviction. I guess he thought the Judge would show more compassion. Boy, was he wrong!

The day of sentencing, many of the jurors come back. They are so irate at what this man has put me and my daughter through that they want to be there to see what the judge does. Of course, Michelle, our friends, my biggest supporter— Barbara, and most of Bevers's family, and I also are here to see what Judge Hopkins will do.

Judge Hopkins has Bevers stand for the sentencing. He tells Bevers he will show the same kind of compassion to him that Bevers showed to his victim. None! He also goes on to say that in all of his years on the bench, this is one of the most brutal rape cases he has ever heard. After lecturing Bevers, he hands him a life sentence, saying he wishes the State provided him an avenue for a more harsh punishment.

He not only gives Bevers life in prison, but hands down a ten-thousand-dollar fine to top it off. Of course, in Texas, a life sentence means about fifteen real years in prison. But it is the fifteen years that I need to start a new life, which means a new identity to hide from Bevers.

Barbara and I hold hands. As the Judge hands down the sentence, I squeeze her little hand so hard it has to hurt her. If it does, she doesn't seem to mind. All we care about is that we have bought me some time, and maybe I can have a life after all.

Jubilant, we sit here for a while. I look at Barbara, give her a huge hug and then hand her the cute, special little doll that has been with me since the hospital. As I let go of what has become my symbol of the innocence and vulnerability of other victims, I say to Barbara, "I've had this doll beside me ever since I was in the hospital. I put her on my nightstand when I got home from the hospital and every night before I went to bed I would look over at her and say, 'We are going to get through this, old girl!' and then I would go to sleep. Well, Barbara, I'm not going to be a victim anymore. She's all yours. You take care of her for me and all of the rest of the victims from now on, okay?"

Barbara flashes a big, beautiful smile at me and says, "You got it!" With that she takes the little doll. She has it with her to this very day.

Chapter 27

Building Bridges

I take the first steps on the road to recovery in that little courtroom when I give Barbara my special little "victim" doll. We hug and rejoice that David and Alan did what everyone said they couldn't...put Lanny Gene Bevers, Jr., away on the rape charge.

The jurors gather around me, hug me, and wish me well. The Judge tells me I am a courageous and strong lady.

Now we will get started with the petitions to keep Bevers behind bars as long as possible. When Barbara and I go to victims' meetings, we carry along our petitions and the members in the club are only too happy to comply by signing. We walk blocks to get signatures. Barbara arranges for me to get in touch with the parole board to send the petitions along with a personal letter pleading for them to keep Bevers in prison as long as possible.

Then I really go to work. I call the Board of Pardons and Paroles, and talk to a parole officer by the name of Pat Keene about Bevers. He tells me he cannot divulge any information to me, but to get in touch with Dan Guerra in Austin, at the State Board of Pardons and Paroles. Not knowing if he is the victim's or the parolee's adversary, I am a little uneasy.

Next, I go to one of the most enthusiastic victims' advocates, Rona Stratton Smith. She provides two names in the parole system through whom she has received information. These two men's jobs consist of getting the data and eligibility dates of inmates coming up for parole.

I do not feel satisfied with these two men, because they indicate to me that they cannot give out any information. The one who is keeping up with the files concerning the inmates' conduct, status, classification, etc., says he could jeopardize his job if he divulges any of this data to me; however, I do manage to get from him that Bevers is in the Coffield Unit in the Tennessee Colony at Palestine, Texas, and that he is certain to be in levels I through VI, depending on his conduct. Parole decisions also will be based on Bevers's past criminal history, the severity of the crime, etc. He will not tell me, though, Bevers's level.

I have a friend, who will remain annonymous, who works dispensing supplies and other data on inmates. The friend looks through the system and tells me that Bevers is taking air conditioning/refrigeration classes and computer-related courses. Out of fear of losing her job, the only thing else she tells me is that

Bevers is in an area slightly more secure than areas for most other prisoners.

I contact Al and Jerry Foster of Victims of Violence and ask if anyone can drive me to Palestine, Texas, to see someone in Commissioner Ken Kasner's office. Next, I have to determine if it is Commissioner Ken Kasner or Cora Moseley of the State Board of Pardons and Paroles who has Bevers's case.

A lady named Ruth drives me to Palestine, Texas. Strangely enough, I want to see where this monster is incarcerated. I know in my heart, if he does not convert to Christianity while in prison, he will make another attempt on my life when he gets out. I then see Commissioner Ken Kasner. Ruth and I both fill out questionnaires as to the purpose of our visit. I enter the commissioner's office alone, and I can't help but notice the deep stacks of inmates' folders that cover his desk. He tells me he respects my position. He says he will take the matter in his care and for me not to worry about a thing. He tells me he will meet with Stennett Posey, another parole board member, and will discuss the matter with him personally.

Upon leaving his office, he shakes my hand and thanks me for coming, while reminding me of the file's process and the time frame.

Victims' rights are still a new phenomenon, and it is unusual for parole board members to meet with victims. A short time later, I receive a call from Mr. Posey. All three members have voted to hold Bevers. Mr. Posey says that they feel Bevers would endanger my life and pose a direct threat if released.

Part III

Taking Control

Chapter 28

The Talk Shows

I am slowly letting it all out. I had kept so much anger in by not wanting to talk about these crimes, until I was called by Rape Crisis and the National Victims' Center and asked if I would be willing to talk about my case in an effort to help others. I reluctantly agree to the first of many interviews and talk shows. It takes me a long time to realize none of this is my fault, and I should not be ashamed. I initially go from silhouetted interviews using a pseudonym finally to a person being interviewed, undisguised, using my real name.

The first interview I agree to is December 11, 1989, with the local NBC affiliate's news program, as an anonymous forty-two-year-old rape victim in silhouette, interviewed by Bernadette Willard.

On April 17, 1990, I am in New York City to appear on the "Jane Wallace Show." The topic of this show is "Rape Victims Speak Out" and is to air the next day. I am once again in silhouette and take on the pseudonym "Joan."

I find myself getting more and more comfortable telling my story, but still have a long way to go. In July 1990, I am taped at the National Victims Center for the Home Shopping Network, local cable TV Channel 49 on the program "In Your Interest." Once again, I adopt the pseudonym of "Joan" in silhouette.

Probably one of the most interesting and exciting offers I have is to appear on the "Oprah Winfrey Show" concerning the topic of "Repeat Rapists." I am initially hesitant, but decide to appear in person with a disguise, still using my pseudonym "Joan." On August 9, 1991, I am in Chicago to film the show, which will air in October on ABC. Barbara watches the show, and is amazed at how her little flower has begun to open up. I speak on a show that millions of people will be watching. That's a scary thought for anyone, but the shows and the telling of my ordeal is a catharsis for me in dealing with my anger.

When I fly back and meet with Barbara, I tell her about some of the lighter moments in the show and how Oprah is very down to earth. My favorite story, I tell her, happens during one of the breaks when a member of the audience suggests castration as an effective means of fighting rapists. Oprah shows her knowledge of the crime when she sits in the makeup chair to get freshened up and says, "Honey, if a man wants to rape you, he'll find a way whether he's got the equipment or not." She understands that rape is a tool for power and control seekers, not seekers of sexual pleasure. In fact, most rapists are impotent. It is the fear in the victim's voice and face that excites them.

I call Barbara one day in March of 1992. I tell her that Channel 5 (the NBC affiliate in Dallas/Fort Worth) is doing a program on "Five Talk Street with Larry McMurray" on gun control. I want her to go with me. Barbara agrees, but says she doesn't plan to speak. She gets angry when a man in the audience suggests that good people shouldn't arm themselves. He says if regular citizens are allowed to own guns we will kill each other off left and right, especially with crimes of passion.

Barbara and her husband, Jim, who is a Tarrant County Sheriff Reserve Deputy, have discussed the show's topic before she leaves. He says in the domestic calls he makes, most of the items used to inflict injury in crimes of passion are regular household items, like irons or the hands of the offender, rather than a gun. Barbara remembers this and speaks up on the show, saying it is time people hold other people accountable for their crimes and not objects, such as guns. "Guns don't kill people; people kill people," she says. I think about the slogan I have seen on the bumper stickers of many Texans' cars: "When guns are outlawed, only outlaws will have guns."

In June 1992, I once again call and ask Barbara if she would like to attend a talk show on Channel 5 called "Spectrum" with host Mike Snyder on "Truth in Sentencing." I know her feelings on this subject, and feel she really can't pass this one up. It is important to her to make sure that the public knows about the real sentence someone does as opposed to the sentence the jurors give them. In Texas a life sentence means fifteen years in prison, no more. That doesn't make sense, and we're trying to get it changed. But prisons cost money, and taxes are usually the way to raise the money to pay for more prisons. I think that people are willing to pay higher taxes if the money is truly used for crime control.

Barbara sees an opportunity to speak up on the show and asks me during the break if she can use my name, show my hand, and explain what happened to me after Bevers was paroled. I say that will be just fine. So after the break Barbara tells Mike and the audience my story. She has never been shy, and I am becoming more and more like her.

In June 1992, I begin work with State Representative Brian McCall in his Anti-Stalking legislation. I am interviewed about stalking by Mary Stewart from Channel 8 News (Dallas/Fort Worth's ABC affiliate). This time I am not in disguise and am not hesitant to use my name, finally realizing who the real criminal is in these matters. No one deserves to be stalked or raped or in any way treated badly by another person.

The next month, Cliff Caldwell with Channel 5 News does a three-day series on stalking. He interviews Barbara and me at length in my home. I do a brief walk-through of the crime. Again, I use my real name. I am prepared to talk about the events in my life openly.

I also do a talk show on Dallas radio station KLIF 570 AM and am interviewed by Ron Lavon on the "Stalking Legislation," which by now is State Representative Brian McCall's House Bill 51.

In August 1992, Barbara and I are asked back to Channel 5's "Five Talk Street" with Barry Simms to discuss the "Anti-Stalking Legislation." State Representative McCall is also there.

My shyness behind me, I talk even longer than Barbara does this time.

I do another interview with local Channel 11 news that same month with Jayna Edwards as I walk her through the crime scene and explain how I had been the victim of a stalker since 1977 (with my only piece of mind being during the six years Bevers was behind bars).

Every appearance from here forward will be on behalf of getting the legislature to pass and the governor to sign an Anti-Stalking Bill.

Chapter 29

Born Again

Barbara has watched me metamorphose from a little cocoon into a beautiful butterfly. Not only am I preparing for my "new birth" with a new name, new location, and new job—I am determined not to have others go through the horror that I have known. I actively join the fight with State Representative Brian McCall and State Senator Mike Moncrief, two very fine men who know this is not a Republican/Democrat issue, but a victim/criminal issue.

State Representative Brian McCall from Plano, Texas, the first to champion my cause, The Anti-Stalking Bill, was elected to the Texas House of Representatives in 1991. He is an outstanding and dedicated young man for whom I feel much affection and respect.

State Senator Mike Moncrief is the second gentleman to get behind my cause. He invites me to a National Victim Center luncheon at the Worthington Hotel in Fort Worth, Texas, on Thursday, April 22, 1993. I feel honored to be invited to sit at the table with the Senator's wife, Rosie, along with some other victim advocacy group leaders. State Senator Moncrief is victim-oriented. He is in Austin at this time regarding the gun control bill.

In working with State Representative McCall and State Senator Moncrief, I do a lot of flying back and forth to Austin—and occasionally other cities—sometimes on short notice, to testify before the House or the Senate, when State Senator Mike Moncrief needs me to testify on the Anti-Stalking legislation.

I testify about my stalking experience before the 73rd Legislature in working with State Representative Brian McCall on Anti-Stalking legislation House Bill 51. State Representative McCall and I first hold a press conference in Austin on Thursday, June 4, 1992, with a briefing at 2:00 P.M. and the conference at 3:00 P.M.

Another press conference is scheduled in Waco, Texas, on Saturday, August 29, 1992, at 2:00 P.M., involving State Representatives Betty Denton and Brian McCall.

I am reimbursed by both the House and Senate for my trips to and from my home in Watauga.

On October 9, 1992, at 2:00 P.M., I participate in a press conference in Amarillo, Texas, along with State Senator Charles Swinford. This will be the last of my press conferences. My next step is to testify before the House of Representatives and the

Senate. I am doing a great job by this time of speaking up in favor of victims' rights.

I testify on behalf of State Senator Mike Moncrief's Anti-Stalking Bill, Senate Bill 25, to the State Senate Jurisprudence Committee on Tuesday, February 9, 1993, at 1:30 P.M., in Committee Room 5. Although nervous and angry, I speak firmly. I am a presence to be reckoned with.

My last testimony takes place upon the request of State House Representative Brian McCall before the State House of Representatives on Monday, February 15, 1993, at 2:00 P.M., in the new annex of the State Capitol. I again speak on behalf of all victims.

House Bill 51 and Senate Bill 25 both pass the House and Senate with flying colors. State Senator Mike Moncrief and State House Representative Brian McCall feel my testimony plays a key role in getting the legislation passed.

I am asked to stand by Texas Governor Ann Richards's side when the Anti-Stalking Bill is signed on March 19, 1993. Texas is the thirty-third state to pass this legislation, and I am there to witness the event. I smile as all the cameras flash while Governor Richards signs the bill, then turns around and hands me the first pen. That pen is prominently displayed in my home with other memorabilia from past talk shows to remind me that God's fingerprints can take me anywhere.

My ordeal has been unique because of the turn of events in my particular case. As a victim, I persevered despite opposition, both on the job and in my personal life, and have gained the admiration and respect of many people—from those I meet on the street to the governor of Texas. I have taken the most negative thing that ever happened in my life and struggled—

sometimes angry—sometimes crying, and turned it into a victory for victims all over the state of Texas.

Someday, Bevers will get out of prison, if he doesn't die in there. To live in peace, I must someday go underground, give up most of these new-found friends, and forge a new identity for myself. I have gone through a government program to get a new name and completely different identity, similar to provisions made by the Witness Protection Program. The victim has to leave behind all he or she has known to ensure future safety. Somehow that just seems to add insult to injury. A victim should never have to hide like the criminal.

No one will know my true name or where I live. I am told my bravery is beyond measure. Barbara confides in me, after all we have been through together, that she can only look on in amazement, as she watches this woman who first came to her so timid and shy, be reborn inside and out.

Chapter 30

Paths that Crossed

During my ordeal I have met some good, kind, and decent people. If you are an upbeat person, as Barbara convinced me I am, you try to find the good in the bad. Some of the people that I met on my journey through the judicial system will always remain special in my heart.

There is Ray Stewart, a gentleman who was minding his own business until he was hurled into the judicial system when his daughter was murdered shortly after my rape. At first, Ray was filled with rage. He did something a lot of people don't have the strength and courage to do: he fought back by joining the system. He became well-known to all the people at the District Attorney's Office and the courthouse, monitoring trials and soothing other victims. He now works full time for Victim

Assistance in the District Attorney's Office. Ray is one of the special ones who took negative energy and turned it into a positive force, helping countless numbers of people in the interim.

Raven Kazen, the director of the Victims Services section of the Texas Department of Criminal Justice, Board of Pardons and Paroles, is another special person. She is a beautiful and compassionate lady with a heartfelt concern for the victims of violence. Like Barbara, she puts her heart and soul into helping victims because it feels good and it is the right thing to do. I happened to meet her when she spoke at an advocate's meeting filled with victims. Raven was instrumental in encouraging me to protest Bevers's release. Raven even took me to a PAVC (People Against Violent Crimes) meeting in Austin.

She and I stood side by side on the steps of the Capitol as Governor Ann Richards addressed victims during National Victims Week in April 1991. She was a great motivator for me. She and Barbara told me some of the same things to do to keep Bevers locked up, which convinced me they must be right.

Patsy Ann Yager Day is another very special lady who is the founder and executive director of Victims Outreach, a non-profit organization that provides emotional and legal support for victims of violent crimes. She founded the organization while she was trying to deal with the loss of her beautiful, teenage daughter who was kidnapped from her place of employment and murdered.

Deborah Caddy is the director of Rape Crisis of Tarrant County. She and Linda Barker-Lowrance of the National Victims Center were instrumental in getting me to do the "Jane Wallace" talk show. That was the program that Nancy Ziggenmeyer of Des

Moines, Iowa, was on. She was one of the first people to come forward with her true identity in her rape case, and she also consulted on a TV movie about her experiences.

David Chapman, assistant chief of the Appellate Section, defies description because he has so many good qualities. He truly believes in victims' rights, and he will fight until there is no fight left in him to see that a wrong is righted. He is a rare prosecutor in that he keeps up with all the victims he "inherits" in the Appellate Section. He not only is their lawyer but becomes their friend as well. I knew from the way Barbara described him to me, before I ever met him, I would really like him.

Texas Governor Ann Richards was first introduced to me when we met for the signing of the Anti-Stalking Bill. I felt modest and commented I only played a small part in the Anti-Stalking legislation, but it only took a minute for State Representative McCall to jump in and say that I had a great deal to do with the passage of this Bill. Governor Richards gently chided me, telling me that she used to downplay her role in events, too. "But, by gosh, if you are instrumental in getting something good done, then stand up and take the credit for it," the Governor told me. When Governor Richards sat down to sign the bill, she whispered to me, "I think we should call this the 'La Vonne Skalias Anti-Stalking Bill,'" then gave me a smile and a wink, and started signing.

These are only a few of the people instrumental in the change in my life and my attitude. There are just too many wonderful people to go into great detail about. I will say that the following people also are important in my life and the contact they had with me on the Anti-Stalking legislation and Victims'

Rights: Al and Jerry Foster; Sharon Mullins; dear Ellen Rosberg, who is now deceased and went through much pain and sorrow from her husband's murder; Rona Stratton Smith; Detective Martin; Linda Braswell; Betty Marshall in the District Attorney's Appellate Section; State Senator Ted Lyon of Rockwall; Victoria Prescott with the law firm of Snyder, Snackerd, and Gambill; State Senator Charles Swinford of Amarillo; State Representative Betty Denton of Waco; State Speaker of the House Gib Lewis; State Representative Bill G. Carter of Richland Hills, Texas; State Representative Doyle Willis of Fort Worth; and Karen Kalargis, director for the Texas Crime Victims Clearinghouse in the Governor's office in Austin; and in particular, a special lady, Loretta, now a Victim's Advocate. Barbara had met Loretta (before I ever knew her), in Kenneth Dies' office, the lead prosecutor in her case and Barbara's close friend, shortly before Loretta's case was to go to trial. Her husband had hired a hit man to rape and then kill her. The hit man turned informant, and Ken Dies was going after the husband on charges of solicitation to commit capital murder. Loretta was scared to death to go to trial. But with Barbara's prodding and Ken's tenacity, along with my support, Loretta felt she could make it through the trial.

Both my trial and Loretta's trial were getting ready to go to court close to the same time. The two of us leaned on each other and gave the other support and courage to face the difficult fights we had ahead. I will never forget this brave, fiery, red-haired lady who helped me when I needed it the most.

Of course, the most special person who came into my life was Barbara. She stood beside me, fought for me, cried with me, and, as far as I'm concerned, saved my life, because she kept forging ahead when everyone else thought the case was a lost cause. She believed in me then and believes in me now. She will be my friend, who I will love dearly for the rest of my life. I know she feels the same way about me.

Epilogue

fter all has been said and done, these are the facts we are left with:

Lanny Gene Bevers, Jr., to this day proclaims his innocence. He is in maximum security in the prison at Coffield Unit, Tennessee Colony, Palestine, Texas. He has refused all requests for any interviews. He will be eligible for parole in January 2005.

Michelle Skalias is now married to a wonderful young man. They live a contented life in an undisclosed location.

La Vonne Skalias is no longer the person she used to be. She is as strong-willed as ever. She champions other victims' causes. Oh, and she is no longer La Vonne Skalias. She lives life as fully as possible with a new identity in an undisclosed location. La Vonne and I remain close friends to this day, but I don't even know her new identity or location, for the protection of both of us. I just want her to be happy wherever she is.

And me, well, I'm still writing. I speak on behalf of victims' rights at different law enforcement agencies and victims' groups. I am also working diligently with Sheriff David Williams's office to establish a Tarrant County Sheriff's Department's Victim Assistance Office.

—Barbara Davis

RAPE

On a hot summer night, a stranger broke into my home.
Having no lover or spouse, my child and I were all alone.

The intruder wore a mask and brandished a butcher knife.
I feared for my child's safety, as well as my very own life.

But the taking of my life was not his main goal, you see.
He wanted to humiliate, degrade, have control of me.

As I obeyed his commands, I couldn't stop crying.
Letting him violate my body was better than dying.

The short time he was with me changed my whole life
    completely.
Once a strong-willed woman, reduced now to a child so meekly.

You're thinking, Is she very pretty, does she wear tight jeans?
Not especially, not really, but then rape's not what it seems.

Rape has nothing to do with the physical act of sex.
Control and power are used to make your mind a total wreck.

I'm fearful of the darkness, and I'm fearful of the light.
I carry a weapon at all times, and stand ready to fight.

This is the real world, my friend, you and I must survive in;
Where the rape of one's mind is almost impossible to mend.

—*Barbara Davis*